Treatment of the Narcissistic Neuroses

Treatment of the Narcissistic Neuroses

HYMAN SPOTNITZ, M.D. Med. Sc.D.

PHYLLIS W. MEADOW, Ph.D.

A Modern Psychoanalytic Publication

FROM THE

*MANHATTAN CENTER FOR
ADVANCED PSYCHOANALYTIC STUDIES*

First published in 1976
Copyright © in 1976 by The Manhattan Center
for Advanced Psychoanalytic Studies
New York, N.Y. 10011
All rights reserved
Designed by David Miller
Printed in the United States of America

Library of Congress Cataloging in Publication Data

Spotnitz, Hyman, 1908–
Meadow, Phyllis W., 1924–
Treatment of the narcissistic neuroses

Bibliographies: p. 235
Includes index

1. Neuroses. 2. Narcissism. I. Meadow, Phyllis W., 1924–
joint author   II.   Title
[DNLM: 1. Narcissism. 2. Personality disorders–
Therapy. 3. Psychoanalytic therapy. WM610 S765t]

RC530.S63   616.8'5   76-6716

ISBN 0-916850-01-3

CONTENTS

ACKNOWLEDGMENTS

I WAS VERY MUCH influenced by a personal analysis with Lillian Delger Powers—an analysis of five years' duration that was conducted five or six times per week. Dr. Powers was instrumental during the course of my own analysis in helping me to deal with all of the emotional problems induced in me by the psychotic patients with whom I was working. She seemed to be a modern psychoanalyst herself, in a sense, since she recognized, when I was talking about the emotional problems of my patients, that I might be talking about the problems they induced in me.

Other influences on the development of modern psychoanalytic ideas came from my work with Rudolf Loewenstein, with whom I trained for about a year; Drs. Herman Nunberg and Sandor Rado, my supervisors for a year or two; Dr. Sarah Bonnett; and finally, in the classroom, Dr. Ludwig Eidelberg. Mark Kanzer, a friend from my years in medical school, was helpful in that I had a sounding board and an enthusiastic discussant as these ideas were developing. Dr. Kanzer is now a psychoanalyst practicing in New York. He and I, with Dr. Louis S. Chase, a Boston psychoanalyst, began talks on narcissism and its treatment at the University of Berlin (1928-34).

Dr. Karl Menninger, who in the late thirties ran

seminars for psychiatric residents in New York City, influenced my thinking, as did Dr. Philip Polatin and Dr. John Rosen, with whom I had many discussions on his treatment of psychotic patients. John Rosen demonstrated time and time again that he had a special skill in dealing with the psychotic state and reversing it so that a patient could become ambulatory and manageable in the analyst's office.

A person essential in the development of modern psychoanalysis was Miriam Berkman Spotnitz, who discussed with me many of the ideas being disseminated by the psychology department of Radcliffe College during the late twenties. Mrs. Spotnitz has been encouraging and understanding up to the present time.

HYMAN SPOTNITZ

*

A NUMBER OF TEACHERS of modern psychoanalysis prepared me for my part in writing this book: Ethel Clevans, Yonata Feldman, and Marie Nelson, with whom I worked when I was in training; Theodor Reik, one of my supervisors, who taught me not to be afraid to follow a great man; and most of all, Hyman Spotnitz, with whom I began my introduction to modern psychoanalysis in 1959. Other factors which played a part in my development as a modern analyst were the timing of my entrance into history and the circumstances of my childhood. I had the advantage of an extended family living together in a small suburb of Boston. Ruby Annis and George Whitcomb, my paternal grandparents, were able to provide the kind of family feeling which I can now experience toward our professional family in psychoanalysis. Learning to love and hate without the need to split these feelings between camps has been the life-long task of our profession.

My arrival at adulthood coincided with a number of notable events in American psychoanalysis. I was a witness to the early developments: the growth of psychoanalytic institute training and the expansion of the frontiers of psychoanalysis to a theory and treatment of all reversible emotional disorders.

For assistance in creating a more readable manuscript I wish to thank Norma Fox Moxley and her copyeditors. To Julia Older Bazer for general editorial assistance, my deepest appreciation. Felix Morrow made invaluable suggestions on the production of this book and found David Miller for us. I am particularly indebted to my family, Cy Meadow, Dena and Jim Reed, George, Jessie and Gladys Whitcomb, Marjorie and Kuno Leaf, Susan and Edward Winbourne for living with me through the many revisions. To Pat Fitzgerald, Judy Landy, Sara Seder and Judy Briggs, who helped in the preparation of this manuscript for printing, many thanks.

PHYLLIS W. MEADOW

For permission to reprint material to which they hold copyright, grateful acknowledgment is made to the following: Psychoanalytic Review published by the National Psychological Association for Psychoanalysis and the psychology department of Stuyvesant Polyclinic. Portions of the chapter on the origins of modern psychoanalysis are a revised version of material that appeared earlier in The Modern Psychoanalysis of the Schizophrenic Patient published by Grune & Stratton.

PREFACE

WITH OUR INCREASING understanding of the psychological reversibility of the narcissistic disorders, the phrase "not suitable for treatment" has been dropped from the vocabulary of the modern psychoanalyst.

The early psychoanalytic method of interpretation and confrontation shifted from explanations of the unconscious impulses to explanations of unconscious defenses. However, this modification was not sufficient to successfully resolve the resistance patterns of the preoedipal personality. Rather, confrontations and clarifications of defensive patterns further corroded the defense structure. The difficulty seemed to be that the weakened ego behind the narcissistic defense was not able to integrate insights into its mode of functioning. An important advance in psychoanalysis as a profession was the development of a method of treatment of narcissistic disorders within the psychoanalytic framework. This volume shows how the early Freudian understanding of libido and aggression was expanded until it could explain preverbal as well as oedipal disorders.

Modern psychoanalysis was developed as a new approach to the study of narcissism. The first time the term "modern psychoanalysis" was used, it was predicted that ultimately the "special approaches being developed for the treatment of the preverbal personality will facilitate the emergence of a more efficient form of psychotherapy for both verbal and perverbal personalities—a modern form of psychoanalysis" (Spotnitz, 1962, p. 3).

In February 1971, ten years after this prediction, a modern psychoanalytic training institute was established and the first two lecture series on modern psychoanalysis were delivered at the New York Academy of Science, under the auspices of the Center for Modern Psychoanalytic Studies. Participants in this series had for ten to twenty-five years been working as modern psychoanalysts in New York.

Modern psychoanalysis, as it is being used here, refers to a specific body of theory and technique developed by Spotnitz, and is distinguished from its general usage to describe developments subsequent to classical theory.

Bernstein (1962) explained modern psychoanalysis in the Foreword to *Paradigmatic Approaches to Psychoanalysis:*

> Modern psychoanalysis takes its point of departure from the problems left unresolved by Freud and his original associates. Interest today is increasingly concentrated on such themes as ego psychology, object relations theory and techniques of treatment. Professional and clinical problems that have plagued psychoanalytic practitioners ever since Breuer retreated in alarm from the violent transference reaction of Anna O. are currently under full discussion [p. 3].

Modern psychoanalysis, as a specific theory and technique, had its roots in an experiment begun in the forties. Under the direction of Yonata Feldman, and with Hyman Spotnitz as consulting psychiatrist, a team of social workers at the Jewish Board of Guardians began work on the "Borderline Project." In the project, caseworkers were assigned borderline and schizophrenic children and their families to investigate why these patients did not respond to the existing treatment approaches. This, as we later learned, was the proper frame of mind to have with narcissistic patients—they were hopeless, the situation was hopeless, and the treatment would probably end in failure. Therapists were helped to undo their own blocks to experiencing narcissism as they explored the nature of the patient's blocks. It was found that the caseworker's resistance to self-understanding was one of the major obstacles to helping in the patient's maturation. The monographs and articles on schizophrenia emanating from the project outlined a new theory of technique for the ego in need of insulation. These articles together cover the early developments in the modern psychoanalytic treatment of schizophrenia.

Now, through an exchange faculty program, modern psychoanalysis is taught in training institutes in New England, New York, Pennsylvania, Florida, Colorado, and California. The modern psychoanalytic approach is an experimental one. It works with the patient-analyst relationship to undo self-destructive responses in the patient. It has made a number of modifications in Freudian theory and technique, most of them based on predicted directions of growth referred to in Freud's later writings.

This text, the first in a modern psychoanalytic series, will review the parallel developments in psychoanalysis in America today. The Introduction surveys the develop-

ment of a theory of aggression from Breuer and Adler
through Spotnitz and the modern psychoanalytic group.
In part one, theoretical considerations in treatment, the
fusion of prefeelings of love and hate to be found in the
narcissistic defense, is described along with two new
concepts: the narcissistic transference and the narcissistic
countertransference. General diagnostic categories are
examined: those in which aggression is internalized, the
narcissistic defense, and those in which the attack is
directed outward, paranoia and mania. Several new developments in dream theory are described and Freud's personal dreams are examined as a way of investigating
preverbal history.

Part Two, Technical Considerations, deals specifically
with analytic intervention and case material to further
explicate the narcissistic personality and its treatment.
Dreams are discussed from the point of view of the
resistance function that they serve. The final chapter
considers recent developments in modern group
psychoanalysis.

THE ORDEAL OF THE HERO

Before Väinamöinen–hero already in his birth–could make his way ashore, the ordeal of a second mother-womb remained to him, that of the elemental cosmic ocean. Unprotected now, he had to undergo the initiation of nature's fundamentally inhuman forces. On the level of water and wind he had to experience again what he already so well knew.

'In the sea five years he sojourned,
Waited five years, waited six years,
Seven years also, even eight years,
On the surface of the ocean,
By a nameless promontory,
Near a barren, treeless country.
On the land his knees he planted,
And upon his arms he rested,
Rose that he might view the moonbeams,
And enjoy the pleasant sunlight,
See the Great Bear's stars above him,
And the shining stars in heaven
　　Thus was ancient Väinamöinen,
He, the ever famous minstrel,
Born of the divine Creatrix,
Born of Ilmatar, his mother.'

Joseph Campbell
1949, p. 301

INTRODUCTION
The Growth of Modern Psychoanalysis

IN RECENT YEARS, psychoanalysts have been considering various means for the resolution of resistances to
the expression of aggressive feelings. Working with
aggression, modern psychoanalysts have concentrated on
the cure of psychologically reversible illnesses, such as
psychosomatic disorders, organic disorders with a psychological component, psychoses, neuroses and character
disorders. As in classical analysis, the modern analyst's
strategy is to create a transference situation by having the
patient communicate verbally from the couch. Cure is
then effected through analysis and resolution of transference resistances—blocks to the expression of repressed
feelings. Modern psychoanalysts have come to think of
cure quite simply as the development of a mature personality capable of thinking and feeling everything.

By focusing on the aggressive drive in the initial
treatment phases and later focusing on the libidinal drive,
the modern analyst attempts to liberate libidinal energy.
The patient is regarded as dominated by the aggressive
drive (Spotnitz, 1969b), with the libidinal source of energy
used for the defense against aggression. Another way of

looking at the same situation is to regard the aggressive drive as developing as a defense against the libidinal drive. To what extent the patient is dominated by the libidinal defenses against the aggressive drive or the aggressive defenses against the libidinal drive is studied in each individual case. In the answer to this question lies the diagnosis and treatment plan.

Freud pioneered the development of the concept of object transference after the phenomenon appeared unexpectedly while he was treating hysterical patients by the cathartic method. Eventually he described it as an unconscious phenomenon operating in all human relations.

When he reported the case of Dora, Freud (1905) described the transference process as:

> a whole series of psychological experiences [which] are revived, not as belonging to the past, but as applying to the person of the physician at the present moment. Some of these transferences have a content which differs from that of their model in no respect whatever except for the substitution. These then are merely new impressions or reprints. Others . . . will no longer be new impressions, but revised editions [p. 115].

An Autobiographical Study (1925), the definitive exposition of Freud's views of transference, contains the clearest statement of his misgivings about negative transference and also is relevant to his views on countertransference:

> Transference is merely uncovered and isolated by analysis. It is a universal phenomenon of the human mind, it decides the success of all medical treatment, and in fact dominates the whole of each person's relation to his human environment . . . when there is no inclination to a

transference of emotion such as this, or when it has become entirely negative, as happens in dementia praecox or paranoia, then there is also no possibility of influencing the patient by psychological means. [p. 42].

In 1909 he indicated his belief that negative transference nullifies the possibility of therapeutic effect. Thus, despite his conviction that the analysis of transference is the core of a successful psychoanalysis and that these transferential impressions exist in all human relationships, Freud could not accept that the person in a negative transference is amenable to psychological treatment.

TOWARD AN UNDERSTANDING OF AGGRESSION

Josef Breuer appears to have been the first psychotherapist to call attention to the existence of the aggressive drive. He made two references to it in the *Studies on Hysteria* (Freud and Breuer, 1895, pp. 201, 264).

Early in the century (1907), Freud maintained the view that, "every act of hate issues from erotic tendencies." (Nunberg and Federn, 1962, p. 164). Freud subsequently stated (1909):

I cannot bring myself to assume the existence of a special aggressive instinct alongside of the familiar instincts of self-preservation and of sex, and on an equal footing with them. . . .I should prefer for the present to adhere to the usual view, which leaves each instinct its own power of becoming aggressive [pp. 140–141].

It was only very late in life that Freud came to

recognize that the aggressive drive was something to be separated from the libidinal drive. In the *Outline of Psychoanalysis* (1940), he mentioned that he had not dealt sufficiently with the problem of the aggressive drive: "All of psychoanalysis has to be reformulated in terms of understanding the aggressive drive as separate from the libidinal drive." Modern psychoanalysts have used this as their starting point.

The pioneer in understanding aggression was Alfred Adler, who, in 1908, postulated the existence of an aggressive drive in a theoretical paper titled "The Aggressive Drive in Life and Neurosis." If Adler had developed this idea further, it might have been possible for him to cure many narcissistic and psychosomatic disorders.

In (1921) Nunberg (1948) reported a case in which he viewed the patient's problem as one of libidinal conflict:

> In a state of narcissistic identification in which there was "no longer a boundary between us" the patient experienced aggressive (cannibalistic) impulses and fantasies of sacrifice. In one situation the patient said, "It seems to me that I am to hit somebody, to tear out somebody's hair." Thereupon he struck his own head with his fist and started to pull out his hair. Here the defense against aggressive impulses was enacted by the instinct turning against his own person and changing into its opposite .... Nevertheless, the aggressive tendency continued to exist beside the passive tendency and even increased in violence [p. 24].

While Nunberg concentrated on the libidinal aspects of the case and explained it in these terms, the patient's words shed a different light on his fundamental problem as it was reactivated in the analytic relationship. His words provide evidence for the theory that destructive impulses toward his primary object were a crucial factor in the illness. In effect he was saying: My desire to preserve you protects you and defends me against my wish to destroy you.

An early illustration of the schizophrenic tendency to direct aggressive impulses against the self was provided by Reik. One of his patients, while in a state of depersonalization, told him : "Instead of knowing that you want to kill someone else, you wipe yourself out."

Rosenfeld (1947) called attention to the same mechanism in the following statement about a schizophrenic woman: "Instead of attacking and destroying the analyst, the destructive impulses had turned against her desire to live, her libido, which left her half dead, as it were, and so in a state of depersonalization."

In one of the earliest attempts to explain the withdrawal from objects, Klein (1930) attributed this withdrawal to the ego's "exaggerated and premature defense against sadism, beginning in the first few months of life." The turning of destructive impulses against the object, which is first expressed in fantasied oral-sadistic attacks on the mother's breast, and later on her entire body, leads to the development of mechanisms regarded as tremendously important for the development of the disorder. In Klein's view, the excessive sadism gives rise to anxiety too severe for the infantile ego to master. Thus the earliest modes of defense are set into action against two sources of danger: The sadism itself and the object, from whom similar retaliatory attacks are feared.

The concept that the aggressive drive destroys the ego unless it has an adequate outlet was described in some detail by Spotnitz (1969b) as it relates to the schizo-

phrenic reaction. The basic pattern is one of the psyche
that clings to the object with libidinal cathexis and obliterates it with aggressive cathexis.

> The integrity of the psyche and the fate of the external
> object are the stakes in the battle between aggressive object
> cathexis fighting for the control of motility and libidinal
> cathexis checking motility to prevent destructive action.
> In these high tension states, libidinal energy is adequate to
> inhibit hostile behavior, but is overwhelmed as the or-
> ganizing force of the mental apparatus. . . .
> This is somewhat akin to smashing a gun to bits to prevent
> oneself from pulling the trigger. The notion that psy-
> chological murder of the object and psychological suicide
> are ways of fighting against the lifting of the barriers of
> actual murder and suicide helps to make the patient's
> behavior and disorder itself comprehensible [1969b, pp.
> 30–32].

To explain this defense Spotnitz wrote:

> The primitive ego was taught—by an object regarded as
> extremely valuable—that the release of aggression was
> undesirable and operated as consistently as possible to
> bottle it up. When this proved impossible, the aggression
> was discharged in a way that would not be harmful to the
> greatly needed real object; instead, it was directed to object
> and egotized object representations in the mind. Growth
> processes were interrupted or reversed by this pathological
> response to undischarged aggression. Its accumulation in a
> stagnant psychic apparatus provides the optimal condition
> for the development of the schizophrenic reaction [1969b,
> p. 31].

Prior to the modern psychoanalytic movement, other

analysts were developing parallel ideas. Sechehaye (1956) believed that the schizophrenic defends himself against the "penetration by someone else" and also against an "eruption of affective and emotional life" through the absence of contact with other persons. Hill (1955) and Schlesinger (1962) added to this concept of the schizophrenic process the ego-sacrifice and frustration factors. And according to Rosen (1963), psychosis serves the basic function of keeping the individual from "recognizing, consciously, the latent source of the terror . . . he experienced with the early maternal environment as he construed it."

NARCISSISM IN THE TRANSFERENCE

It was Waelder who in 1924 introduced the concept and use of narcissistic transference as a technical term. He proposed a method of treatment oriented toward sublimation of narcissism and described a case in which a transference of that nature proved sufficient to sustain the relationship. Clark (1926) described a "fantasy method" of analyzing the narcissistic neuroses and characterized such transference as the "mother type," contrasting it with the "lover type" that evolves in the transference neuroses. Aichhorn (1948) found he could therapeutically influence a young delinquent who was unable to form a meaningful object relationship except through an "overflow of narcissistic libido" by presenting himself as a glorified replica of the patient's delinquent ego and ego-ideal. This was probably the first description of the ego-syntonic object transference. Bak (1939), another early advocate of such functioning, recommended that the therapist should "represent a narcissistic object so that he would appear to the patient as a part of himself."

Among other isolated references to narcissistic transference in the 1930's and 1940's were those of Stern (1938) and Cohn (1940). Stern offered specific recommendations for working with patients who present "painfully distorted narcissistic transference reactions." Cohn described rudimentary and primitive transference reactions and their manifestations. Of special interest is Cohn's observation that the patient at times "refers to the analyst when he speaks of himself and vice versa." Rosenfeld (1947) reported that a particular type of object relationship developed in all cases of schizophrenia which he treated: "As soon as the schizophrenic approaches *any* object in love or hate, he seems to become confused with this object." Freeman (1963) described the details of a case in which an "intensive positive" narcissistic transference led to an intractable "resistance of idealization." Searles (1963) has described transference psychosis as "any type of transference which distorts or prevents a relatedness between patient and therapist as two separate, alive, human and sane beings." Little (1958) introduced an analogous concept when she described a transference state in which the analyst "*is*, in an absolute way,...both the idealized parents and their opposite, or rather, the parents deified and diabolized, and also himself (the patient) deified and diabolized." She called this delusional transference (p. 134).

Balint (1952) in conceptualizing transference as a "new beginning," wrote that

> Some patients regress to primitive stages in their development, in order to begin the process of adaptation anew ...

Primitive, undifferentiated states are elastic, capable of new adaptation in various directions ... if a radical new adaptation becomes necessary, the highly differentiated organization must be reduced to its primitive undifferentiated form from which a new beginning may then be made [p. 214].

Lagache (1953) described transference as the "activation of an unsolved conflict; injury to the narcissistic drives ... is not just a reason for defense, it evokes an unconscious demand for reparation" [p. 1]. Elaborating on the need-fulfilling function of various transference states, Meerloo and Nelson (1951) refer to negative transference as the "patient's quest for a means of handling negative feelings." Klein (1952) expressed the view that transference originates in object relations of the first year of life and reflects the presence of hatred as well as love, or "the mechanisms, anxieties, and defenses operative in the earliest infancy." Bullard advised against attempting to establish positive transference when beginning treatment with a patient who has rarely experienced "warm and uncomplicated" interpersonal relationships because an approach that "assumes that [the patient] has had these experiences is doomed to failure."

Other writers have expressed similar views: for instance, L. Bryce Boyer and P.L. Giovacchini (1967) wrote that, "The schizophrenic is terrified of the potential destructiveness of his impulses and when the emergence of hatred of former love objects is discouraged, he thinks the therapist fears his own or the patient's hostility."

THE NARCISSISTIC DEFENSE

So far we have discussed the people who have contributed to the pragmatic understanding of the role of aggression, object protection and sacrifice of the ego in connection with the narcissistic defenses, and also those who have helped to develop the concept of transference. The following originators of modern psychoanalysis have worked successfully with the aggressive impulses in the treatment of psychotic states. Interestingly, one of the first to deal successfully with psychotic states was Josef Breuer (L. Freeman, 1972), who treated Bertha Pappenheim (Anna O.) with hypnosis and "talking cure"; after several relapses Anna O. was relieved of her psychosis. Freud adopted Breuer's method and from it developed the system of psychoanalysis which eventually became classical psychoanalysis. But, as we have seen, Freud did not have the idea until late in his life that psychotic states could be treated successfully in psychoanalysis. A.A. Brill (1949) quoted Freud as having said that he finally thought that psychoanalysis could hope to eventually cure psychotic states. Bjerre (1911), another pioneer in the field, reported the successful treatment of a paranoid psychotic woman.

The prognosis for schizophrenia, as the years went by, improved continually and today one gets the impression that as we understand the schizophrenic process better, as as more results are reported, the prognosis will improve even more. A number of people have been successful in applying modern ideas to the treatment of schizophrenia and to the investigation of the schizophrenic process.

Among those who have reported favorable results with schizophrenia is Karl Menninger, who originally was extremely pessimistic about treating schizophrenics. He pointed out in *The Human Mind* (1945): "It is now well recognized that this dread disease is by no means hopeless, granted the availability of prompt and skillful treatment."

Arieti (1961) also contributed to the slowly rising curve of optimism about schizophrenia: "It is possible to offer the schizophrenic some methods by which he may ... lose his symptomatology and orient himself toward a more productive, mature and nonpsychotic life."

Fromm-Reichman (1952) found that when it seemed impossible to establish a workable doctor-patient relationship with a schizophrenic patient, the problem was attributable to "the doctor's personality difficulties, not to the patient's psychopathology."

Although Sechehaye (1956) used psychotherapy with schizophrenic patients, her theory is difficult to apply because it does not focus on personality dynamics. She conceptualized the theraputic process as one of meeting the need for discharge of impulses but neither distinguished between erotic and aggressive impulses nor addressed the defense against impulse discharge.

Zilboorg (1931) analyzed a young woman suffering from paranoid schizophrenia and identified the nucleus of her psychosis as an "early infantile conversion" in which the patient displaced her hatred of her parents onto herself. The severe frustration she experienced at the age of five "dammed up an enormous mass of instinctual energy which produced or activated her hostile impulses to the utmost degree" (p. 493). It was Zilboorg's impression that these impulses were permitted to break through only when she was in a psychotic state.

Hendrick's article on the psychoanalysis of a schizo-phrenic young woman on the verge of psychosis (1931) is an outstanding study of an "immature ego endangered by aggressive impulses." Hendrick attributes the inability of the patient's ego to repress infantile sexual impulses to the fact that the available energy "was mobilized in the service of another function, namely, the control of enormous impulses of aggression."

According to Bak (1954),

> The sudden inability of the ego to neutralize aggression (which inherently means the loss of the object in varying degrees) turns the entire aggressive drive loose, and this develops increasing emphasis and destroys the self that has become its object [p. 129].

In some cases, "the ego regresses to its undifferentiated phase or employs other defenses such as projection or withdrawal to avoid the destruction of objects."

When working with schizophrenia the problem seems to be to determine whether the schizophrenic can be cured by the classical technique. Some maintain they have been able to do so. Others who do not use the classical technique seem to be practicing psychotherapy. The important point is that the modern psychoanalyst does not use psychotherapy but works with transference resistance in order to resolve it. Modern psychoanalysis can work successfully with the schizophrenic patient because it has the capacity to deal successfully with transference relationships and resistances.

THERAPEUTIC TECHNIQUE

A number of practitioners can be identified as the precursors of modern psychoanalytic technique. As early as 1936 Jung viewed the analytic process as the "reciprocal reaction of two psychic systems." Annie Reich (1951) claimed that countertransference is a necessary prerequisite for effective treatment, and Gitelson (1952) expressed the view that countertransference reactions "exist as facts in any analysis .... [To the extent that the therapist is] open to their analysis and integration, he is in a real sense a vital participant in the analysis with the patient" [p. 1]. Rosenfeld (1964), Winnicott (1958), and Searles (1965) have also contributed to the body of knowledge about countertransference. Winnicott and Searles apparently recognized that the patient's problems induce similar problems in the analyst. Alexander (1961) was influential in developing some of the notions connected with feelings in modern psychoanalysis. His ideas about constructive emotional experience represent one of his most important contributions to modern psychoanalysis. Many feelings created in the analyst when he works with psychosomatic patients have proved to be significant when used with such patients in office practice, and it has been found that psychosomatic conditions and organic disorders are accessible to the psychological approach.

Modern psychoanalysis has engaged in much research on organic and psychosomatic cases. At present, modern psychoanalysts are trying to formulate new theories that will help the therapist understand schizophrenic, narcissistic, and psychosomatic patients and enable him to treat each of them successfully. There are many theories of human personality and development which may be correct. What modern psychoanalysis tries to develop are theories that, when applied to the patient, help to cure him. Any theory that enables the analyst to understand the patient, but then becomes a detriment to curing him, is discarded. Modern psychoanalysis accepts and works with pragmatic concepts. It does not limit itself to psychological treatment alone. However, although the analyst cooperates with physicians who use physical and chemical methods with patients, he relies only on psychological communication to resolve transference resistances that interfere with mature, healthy functioning.

All psychological methods are included in modern psychoanalysis: e.g., group therapy; individual sessions that range in number from one per year to as many as six per week; and treatment of one patient by several therapists or treatment of several patients by one therapist. In other words, dynamic methods are used singly or in combination with other methods as long as they will help resolve transference resistance, i.e., produce a mature personality. The methodological area is still open to research, and no one knows as yet what the limits to modern psychoanalysis will be.

Many early modern analysts who practiced what they called psychotherapy were intuitively trying to resolve transference resistances but did not recognize their work as transference analysis. We may credit them with being pioneers, though they themselves were not aware that resolving resistance was what they were trying to do. However, they used the methods intuitively that we use deliberately today when trying to resolve transference resistance.

Finally, central to the development of modern psychoanalysis are patients who have worked with modern psychoanalysts. These patients have made important contributions by their improvement and through their suggestions. They have demonstrated to the modern analyst the potential of modern psychoanalysis. Many failures have been caused by the analyst's inability to provide proper psychological interventions. Many successes have been related to patients' suggestions about how analysts should intervene to help them resolve their resistances. When the analyst uses his patients as his guide, his treatment plan itself produces growth. Apparently, modern psychoanalysis owes its successes to patients in the same way that Breuer owed to Anna O. his success in dealing with her.

PART I

Theoretical Considerations in Treatment

It is not only that there is no hiding place for the gods from the searching telescope and microscope; there is no such society anymore as the gods once supported . . . the hero-deed to be wrought is not today what it was in the century of Galileo . . . the modern hero-deed must be that of questing to bring to light again the lost Atlantis of the co-ordinated soul.

Joseph Campbell
1949, p. 388

EROS AND THANATOS:
The Prefeelings of Love and Hate

SCHOOL CHILDREN read the Greek myths as delightful stories about imaginary people. They learn from the dictionary that the very word "mythical" means nonexistent, or the opposite of factual. Then when they grow up and read about modern psychoanalysis, they are told the opposite; that the gods and demigods of ancient Greece behaved very much like themselves.

Myths survive because they echo the universal aspects of our own experience. They drive home some truths about the forces that influence our lives by endowing these forces with human form and personality; they anthropomorphize the realities of life and mirror its major perplexities in symbols that the mind can easily understand.

Eros and Thanatos broadly personify opposite extremes in human behavior. In this sense, they are also identified with conflicting emotional tendencies that influence our behavior as we move from one biological pole of life to the other. The name of the Greek god of love is a familiar symbol of creative living and its fruits—biological, artistic and scientific creativity, and other expressions of human productivity. The name has a welcome sound because Eros is linked with the idea of the good life and its preservation. On the other hand, the word Thanatos evokes negative emotions in most people because he was the Greek god of death. Besides personifying the end of individual existence, Thanatos also encompasses those life-in-death forces and explosions of hatred that threaten human survival—war, genocide, and all the other things we delicately refer to as man's inhumanity to man.

However, the ancient Greeks did not picture Thanatos as such a baleful figure. Homer identified him as the twin brother of Hypnos, the god of sleep. In a sculpture of Olympus, they are two boys sleeping side by side, Hypnos robed in white and Thanatos in black. Euripides gave Thanatos a part in his drama *Alcestis,* and he appeared on the stage with wings of black added to the black garment.

Despite his black accessories, Thanatos enjoyed a relatively good public image in his own myth-time. The ancient Greeks regarded his influence as being limited to the body. Thus, it was not wholly negative since corporeal death liberated the soul to begin a new life. One of Plato's best-known Dialogues develops the idea that living and dying are complementary processes, much like sleeping and waking.

Speculative thinkers of later times have also viewed Thanatos with equanimity, if only because he helped them put on their thinking caps. For example, Schopenhauer advanced the notion that "all philosophy starts in the contemplation of death." This idea has also inspired some immortal poetry.

Scientists , however, rarely mention Eros and Thanatos. They prefer to couch their ideas about human experiences in terms of laws and principles. To illustrate, we quote: "Two contrary laws seem to be wrestling with each other nowadays, the one a law of blood and death ever imagining new means of destruction . . . the other a law of peace, work and health ever evolving new means of delivering man from the scourges which beset him." That statement is so expressive of our contemporary concern that one may be surprised to hear that it was made by the nineteenth century French chemist and bacteriologist to whom we are indebted for the purity of our milk.

When Louis Pasteur died in 1895, Sigmund Freud was a thirty-nine-year-old Viennese neurologist emerging from obscurity with the publication of his first major report on emotional disorders—the *Studies on Hysteria*, written with Josef Breuer. Freud had been reading the Greek poets and philosophers since his high school days. He was sufficiently at home in the language to read Homer in the original, to translate some verses of Sophocles, and to write his own diary in Greek. He sometimes addressed his own daughter, Anna, as Antigone, a name he borrowed from the Oedipus myth. Ideas as well as names derived from the classical mythology are reflected in his writings, and he was influenced by Plato's theory of reminiscence.

It was, therefore, as natural for Freud to attach the nomenclature of myths to his theories as it is for other scientists to formulate theirs as laws and principles. His allusions to Greek antiquity have so strongly influenced the behavioral sciences that one of his theories is still identified with Eros and Thanatos. It is also known as the instinct theory because Freud eventually came to the conclusion that the forces he linked with these names are the basic instincts of life.

Freud's postulates on the aggressive instinct, around

which much current thinking on the subject clusters, were delayed another quarter of a century by his reluctance to identify aggression as a basic human drive. He viewed life and sexual instincts operating under the banner of Eros as:

> ... always trying to collect living substances into ever larger unities, whereas the instinct of Thanatos ... acts against that tendency and tries to bring living matter back into inorganic condition. At times these forces become fused, but by and large they oppose each other. At times, too, the biological tendency toward destruction is deflected from the self. When directed toward other people or things in the external world, it becomes the aggressive instinct, operating constructively as well as destructively [1920, p.7].

In *Civilization and Its Discontents* (1930), Freud wrote, "I can no longer understand how we can have overlooked the ubiquity of non-erotic aggressivity and destructiveness." In 1937, two years before his death, he wrote to Marie Bonaparte, "The whole topic has not yet been treated carefully, and what I had to say about it in earlier writings was so premature and casual as hardly to deserve attention or consideration."(Jones, 1957, p. 464.)

Freud was pessimistic about the ability of Eros to preserve living things. He came to think of Eros, each fresh excursion into life, as a "detour" that served to delay man's return to an inorganic state. Death is one of our most democratic institutions, but the theory that we are born with drives that propel us toward death is not generally accepted. Because of its implications for the forward march of civilization and the future of the human species, the theory has become a debatable issue in all branches of science concerned with the nature and future of man. The theory has also been a source of controversy among Freud's own followers. In this connection, it should be pointed out that the assumption of an instinct toward self-destruction is a biological theory, and it is not possible to validate or disprove a biological theory with psychological evidence alone.

Psychoanalysts who tend to accept the theory function with patients in the same way as those who do not accept it. A practitioner who was intellectually convinced, and operated on the conviction that certain self-destructive tendencies of a patient were irreversible, might not be helpful in dealing with those tendencies. However, the analyst's training and professional identity testify to his belief that such tendencies are responsive to external influence. The acceptance of a case signals the analyst's belief that the patient is capable of mastering these difficulties and that the analyst can help him do so. In other words, whether or not there is an inborn drive toward destruction, is of no particular significance for treatment.

The instinct theory is related only tangentially to Freud's development of psychoanalytic therapy, and he himself made relatively little reference to this theory in his clinical studies. In his later years he became interested in developing a systematic explanation of the destructive tendencies he observed in people, and his assumptions about Eros and Thanatos came within the frame of scientific inquiry. He was well into his sixties when he enunciated his final instinct theory.

We are not interested in making a case for or against the theory. The views expressed here are based solely on observations of severely disturbed patients, and we have not observed an instinct in any of them. What has been observed is that these people often operate in ways contrary to their own best interests. This self-destructive behavior could be instinctual or it could spring from various random sources, such as social training; psychological needs for love, attention, and approval; and other motives. When the pattern of behavior is examined in different perspectives, it may turn out to have constructive, as well as destructive aspects. How it is evaluated depends on the observer's point of view.

As we observe such behavior and speculate on the unknown factors that motivate it, we find that no one theory about it fits all cases. In each case, an assumption is developed which, in due time, is discussed with the patient. The crucial issue is not the correctness of the assumption, but whether it will be helpful to the patient in effecting his giving up the destructive behavior. If a theory does so, it is assumed correct. But if a theory does not help a patient to understand and change his behavior, it is of no value to him, so it can be discarded and other working hypotheses can be developed.

In this process, patients disclose impulses, thoughts, and feelings which, if acted on, would get them into all sorts of trouble. Some patients reveal fears of death and become aware of forces which they say pull them to it. Overpowering urges to harm their loved ones are also disclosed. People think of committing suicidal and murderous acts. If we really do come into the world with this potential, it is all for the best that we arrive as helpless infants. This gives us time to learn to work out basic impulses before we grow strong enough to act on them destructively.

Patients usually talk more freely about their urges to act when they approve of them and believe others will approve. At times the impulses they regard as monstrous, and would prefer to conceal, make it hard for them to act on their so-called good urges. The interplay of these contrary impulses frequently threatens their emotional equilibrium. If Freud had conceptualized Eros and Thanatos in terms of impulses, urges, or emotional tendencies instead of instincts, his views about them would probably have aroused less controversy. People experience impulse currents whose claims for expression do pull them in opposite directions.

Eros and Thanatos symbolize the emotional components of these contrary currents—love and hate. Strictly speaking, Eros and Thanatos are not love and hate per se, but the potential at birth to feel them. This potential varies from infant to infant; it is constitutionally determined. But the earliest training a human being gets in handling these emotional forces largely dictates what kind of equipment his mind will organize to utilize this potential.

It takes several months for this "feeling" equipment to come into existence. During that pre-feeling period, a baby is incapable of perceiving anything beyond sensations impinging on him from the outside world and from his own bodily organs. When he develops actual feelings, their nature and the particular patterns he forms for releasing the feelings reflect the influence of the person who is caring for him. The presence of someone who loves and responds appropriately to a baby's needs stimulates feelings of being loved, and these in turn arouse the child's own love feelings. If, on the other hand, a baby is permitted to remain cold or wet or hungry for unduly long periods, tensions develop which the infant is able to discharge only in part—for example, through wailing or kicking. If such frustrating situations are ended by the proper attention of the mother, his tensions are relieved; if not, the infant experiences rage. If his distress signals are not interpreted correctly, his bout with frustration may be prolonged. One patient recalls with much discomfort that a bottle was stuck into her mouth every time she cried.

The seeds of hate sprout into hate feelings when a young child is mishandled; but what the child does with these feelings depends to some extent on what his mother wants him to do with them. If he senses that she disapproves of outbursts of rage, he will tend to cope with it in some other way, especially if her approval is hard to come by. An emotionally deprived child will go to great lengths to convince himself that his mother loves him or to safeguard the little love she gives him. Severely disturbed people have explained that this unconscious activity begins with the shutting off of feelings. They characteristically shut them off, substituting states of affectlessness—a pattern which is associated with schizophrenia.

When a patient is able to feel his hate impulses rather than his anxiety about them, and when his resistance to discharging them is resolved, it is not the persons for whom he originally felt these destructive urges, but the person conducting treatment who is in the direct line of fire. This is not a purely rhetorical statement. The key to effective, and mutually safe treatment is the activation of these emotional forces in the therapy situation without giving the patient immediate or justifiable cause to hate the analyst. The more the patient feels his aggressive impulses and expresses them in words charged with genuine emotion, the more aware he becomes of his love impulses and the easier it is for him to act on them unobstructedly in healthful and socially constructive ways.

We do not want to leave the impression that verbal discharge of aggression in itself is the crucial factor in reversing pathology. *It is not.* Verbal discharge relieves the patient temporarily, gives him the kind of relief a constipated person experiences when a cathartic works effectively. However, a cathartic is not a curative in the sense of preventing the constipation from recurring. The analogy seems appropriate, particularly in schizophrenia, which is a kind of psychological constipation in which the evacuation of aggressive impulses is extremely difficult and painful. Emotional catharsis alleviates this problem for a time, but the patient has to learn to function so that the problem will not recur. Liberating him from his damaging patterns of bottling up aggressive impulses is the important aspect of treatment. He also has to be helped to develop new patterns for controlling and regulating the discharge of these impulses.

Some of our difficulties in understanding and working with the aggressive impulse can be traced back to the fact that hate is not recognized as a normal emotion. The attitude that it is abnormal and sinful to hate reflects to some extent the inadequacies of parental training. Many children are inculcated with the idea that they are monsters if they feel hate, especially for those they love. A child who is not helped to accept hate impulses as part of his birthright often interprets a parent's disapproval of damaging expressions of these impulses as disapproval of the impulses themselves.

We have found that patients get nowhere trying to run away from the existence of hate. It exists together with love in every psyche. The expression of hatred is a psychological need. That is, it is a desire or wish that presses for satisfaction. No person really lives in an emotionally healthful way until he has developed the capacity to give balanced expression to love and hate. In brief, we need to recognize that the problem is not hate itself, but its expression in harmful ways.

There is no situation in life in which we are justified in forbidding freedom of feeling and thought to Thanatos. Aggressive impulses are always feelable and thinkable. Unfortunately, people do not agree on what is desirable in the expression of negative feelings.

CONCLUSION

Our general approach is based on the hypothesis that the fundamental problem of the pathologically narcissistic patient is the destructive impulse. Although many investigators point to anxiety as his basic problem, that is not the impression gained from working with schizophrenic and other autistic patients for many years. The anxiety is merely the warning that destructive forces are accumulating and putting the person under extreme pressure to act out his urge to destroy.

If one moves back far enough in the history of such a patient, it usually becomes clear that he suffered a particularly damaging failure in the process of maturation. His aggressive energy, lacking outlets for release in feelings and language, was turned back upon the nuclei of his own ego. Aggressive urges are an explosive force, while an inhibiting role is played by libidinal or binding urges. The defense operates unconsciously to protect the object from the release of volcanic aggression, but it serves to disrupt the psychic apparatus.

When effectively treated, Eros and Thanatos are complementary forces. We need the energy which both offer. By releasing the impulse to love from the impossible task of blotting out the impulse to hate, and by taming hate into personally and socially desirable forms of human expression, we diminish the destructive potential of Thanatos and liberate Eros for creative service to all mankind.

DIAGNOSIS RE-EVALUATED

PATIENTS BRING to treatment different ways of perceiving their early environment. The impressions they give us through their productions will tell us whether their earliest reactions to environmental stress tended to be somatic, schizophrenic, or depressive. Some patients attack the body and develop physical symptoms. At the earliest stages of stress, bodily symptoms tended to be the likeliest choice of defense. According to modern analysts, the somatization syndrome is a means of turning aggression against the physical self, and, as we know, medicine increasingly recognizes somatic illnesses as functionally related to psychogenic factors.

PREVERBAL CONFLICTS

The preoedipal or preverbal patient's difficulties relate to maturational failures in the first years of life—in some cases, the first two years of life and possibly intrauterine life. The popular belief that intrauterine life is a paradise in which the fetus floats in amniotic fluid at body temperature, receiving the proper amount of stimulation, led to the belief that childbirth is equivalent to being cast out of paradise. And, indeed, Frederic LeBoyer, a Canadian obstetrician, observed that most infants showed physical signs that they were unhappy to be born. But LeBoyer, dissatisfied, raised the following question:

Why, since prior to birth the infant is buffeted about in utera while the mother goes about her various activities for nine months, as the space to live in gradually becomes smaller and smaller until finally his size forces him to leave the uterus and the infant is squeezed down a canal accompanied by more buffeting, squeezing and tension-inducing sounds, why is it not a great relief to be born? What are we doing wrong, what is the environment doing wrong, to make the post-birth period such an unpleasant experience for the baby?

LeBoyer asked a number of other questions: What confronts the baby as he bursts forth into the new world? Bright lights shining down on him, hurting his eyes and skin. Then the umbilical cord is cut. He gasps for air until he is spanked, and the air rushes into his lungs for the first time—another terrifying experience. And finally, he is wrapped in a cloth, which feels unpleasant on his sensitive skin. On closer examination, LeBoyer asked what does the baby have to be pleased about?

As a result of his questions, LeBoyer began to improve the conditions for the newborn. He experimented with dim lights. He placed the infant on the mother's belly without cutting the umbilical cord and waited until breathing occurred naturally and became regular. Only then did he cut the umbilical cord and submerge the infant in a warm bath, massaging its head while holding it gently on his hand. He waited until the infant was relaxed, playfully kicking his feet, and smiling, before he wrapped it in cloth.

The moments of birth are a torment that condition the infant to fear the future— or, in language a baby would understand, creates bundles of body tension. The damage that leads to the narcissistic disorders seemingly occurs either through our lack of understanding about the infant's needs or through our inability to cope with his demands; thus, we cannot provide him with the proper environment.

LeBoyer has taught us that when a patient comes to us suffering from preoedipal conflicts, we are confronted with a problem similar to the one he faced. If we can understand what it is between mother, child, and the environment that leads to maturity, then we should be able to provide the appropriate treatment environment in which to help our patients mature. The analyst must ask, how the environment has failed to provide this person with what he needed to overcome his anxieties and destructive impulsiveness sufficiently to fulfill his own potential.

In *Project for a Scientific Psychology* (1899) and in the opening pages of *Beyond the Pleasure Principle* (1920), Freud emphasized that the infant's first efforts are directed toward keeping himself impulse-free— that is, the earliest structure is a reflex apparatus which carries sensory excitation to the motor path. Freud's economic and dynamic theories were an elaboration of the basic premise that the ebb and flow of excitation leads to the creation of symptoms, dreams, and verbal slips as indirect forms of discharge. He viewed early ego functions as learned ways of coping with infantile sources of excitation to escape from unpleasure. Seeking discharge of unpleasurable sensation led to primary process thinking.

Recently, Escalona (1974) reported her observations of what appeared to be conscious intent in three-week-old infants who searched for the pleasurable tactual stimulation they had previously experienced by touching a soft blanket. Evidently, the cognitive structure emerges to help the infant discharge his drives and differentiate between his perceptions of self and other. A person regresses to mnemic (early) traces of pleasure to discharge tension symbolically in a manner that at an earlier time was his best way of coping with frustration.

In his search to eliminate unpleasure, an infant may cling to the fantasy of a satisfying breast despite the fact that no milk is forthcoming. Eventually, however, frustration leads him to fantasies of destruction. Psychological research has demonstrated that frustration mobilizes aggression. And if the infant's aggressive energy is not redirected to the motor system, the cumulative tension in the mental system lays down discharge pathways that will overwhelm the structure.

The baby seeks pleasurable or tension-reducing experiences, primarily connected with bodily comforts. When he is frustrated and in a state of helpless rage, destructive impulses may flood the ego. Tension-reducing defenses may also be directed against acknowledging unpleasant affects such as helplessness, inadequacy, or hopelessness. We speak of the pre-object period of infant omnipotence when, it is assumed, a baby is unable to differentiate his own pre-ego feelings from the reality of others. In his omnipotent state the infant attempts to destroy the source of unpleasure but can only attack the internal visual memories of feeding–images that cannot provide the needed satisfaction.

Today we are confronted with an abundance of persons who combine the somatic and socially deviant modes of turning their aggression inward, methods that may not appear to be so obvious a self-attack. Combinations of the somatic and deviant reactions are often seen in alcoholics or drug addicts. The person who attacks himself with alcoholism, drug addiction, or in other ways turns against his physical being is using an early-learned weapon to protect the object and blame himself. Recovery is more difficult in these cases because the illness itself provides secondary gains. Thus these patients must not only get in touch with the feelings warded off in depression and schizophrenia but give up the pleasure they gain from their activities. Only when a patient is able to control his impulses can treatment allow his feelings to come to full bloom in the transference. Then, despite the intensity of his feelings, he will be able to verbalize his destructive impulses rather than act on them.

THE SCHIZOPHRENIC REACTION

In other cases it is the ego that is attacked. The patient may say, "I am confused" or he may speak in a fragmented way as his cognitive functions–thought, judgment, perception–begin to deteriorate. When this happens, we speak of the schizophrenic reaction, in which relationships are protected at the sacrifice of contact with reality. Schizophrenia, an intricately structured but psychologically unsuccessful defense against destructive behavior, apppears to be patterned during the undifferentiated phase of development when ego and object representations overlap.

In the conflict between aggressive wishes and the desire to preserve the object image, the cost is the destruction of feeling and thought processes. The individual is immobilized by this disintegration and loses touch with what he feels. Although this defense has many secondary consequences, the three primary ones are aggression against the mental functioning, object protection, and sacrifice of the self.

For patients who were severely deprived early in life, this response may have been the only means of regaining equilibrium. For example, infants sleep to block off external realities and avoid pain. The history of this defense can be described as follows: If a gratifying image has been replaced in the memory by an image of a depriving person, the desire to annihilate the bad image presumably follows. The orally regressed psyche clings to visual images of early figures with libidinal longing and obliterates them with aggressive destructiveness. In this case, the intrapsychic picture is one of libidinal, or positively charged energy used to defend against the negatively charged energy that creates the wish to destroy the object of libidinal attachment. The patient who uses withdrawal is likely to terminate treatment if he cannot limit the amount of stimulation he receives through this withdrawal. The patient who defends himself by destroying his mind usually does not want to establish an analytic relationship in which strong feelings for the analyst will be aroused. He wants treatment and may hope that he will be made comfortable in the analytic session. If he stays in treatment, he may hope that the analyst will tell him something that will enable him to leave and that everything will then be all right. But he certainly does not want to be emotionally involved in reexperiencing earlier frustrations and deprivations that will arouse fantasies of rage and annihilation and in turn arouse his fears of destructive action.

The link between the schizophrenic reaction and self-hatred is a rather recent psychiatric discovery. Over twenty years ago, it was commonly believed that the primary problem in narcissism was self-love. In treatment the schizophrenic was approached as a person who had withdrawn into a world of his own because he found the people in his real world unlovable. The notion that he was satisfied to love himself in this fantasy world seemed to account for the difficulty of persuading him to return to the world of reality.

Some practitioners still maintain this view of schizophrenia—they base treatment on the idea that the primary need of the patient who behaves this way is compensation in the analysis for earlier emotional deprivation, and that satisfaction of this need will help the patient love others and commit himself to a more sociable way of life.

Because the schizophrenic is an emotionally deprived individual, the analyst's impulse is to respond to his suffering with kindness. When starting out with the schizophrenic patient, many practitioners believe they should give him support, sympathy and encouragement. After listening hour after hour to the schizophrenic patient's descriptions of his strange feelings and the mysterious voices he hears, the analyst may become anxious and attempt to relieve himself of these feelings by trying to soothe the patient.

Experience has taught us, however, that this type of treatment does not help the schizophrenic recover. The schizophrenic patient responds to a sympathetic approach by developing a warmly positive attachment, and the more attached he becomes the more schizophrenic he becomes. In other words, his customary defenses become even more entrenched to guard against the release of hostility. It should be noted that this pattern of behavior is involuntary and compulsive, not deliberate. Few patients are aware that they bury their aggressive impulses or why they are doing so.

One of the earliest clues to this problem was discovered by Spotnitz during his residency in a psychiatric institution. His patient was an attractive young woman, a bride of several months, who was hospitalized following a psychotic episode. In her acute catatonic state, she blotted out her feelings. She did not even feel pain when a cigarette stub burned her fingers; the stubs had to be taken from her.

Several hours a day, five to seven days a week, Spotnitz listened to her sympathetically, tried to draw her out, and laughed with her at her own wisecracks. Nothing significant happened, however, until he said a few harsh words to her. She instantly responded by hurling a glass ashtray at him, missing his head by inches. The miss, she said later, was intentional; but she had really felt like killing him. Spotnitz helped her to accept the idea that she was entitled to vent her rage as often as she wished, provided that she exploded in feelings and words instead of throwing things. At this point, the patient began to improve.

Eventually, it became clear that her initial psychotic episode had been precipitated by rage at her husband. About a month before the breakdown, she had undergone an abortion because she believed her husband had tricked her into an unwanted pregnancy. Extensive treatment in childhood and adolescence, combined with the fact that her illness was acute and recent rather than chronic, helped to account for her rapid progress in treatment. She was able to talk out her hostility within six months and was discharged from the hospital as recovered. We attribute her subsequent recovery to the fact that she stopped defending herself against her hatred and learned how to feel it and verbalize or release it in appropriate behavior.

Another clue to the basic problem was furnished by a schizophrenic woman whom Spotnitz treated some years ago. Her associates regarded her as a pleasant, placid person, who kept to herself. When she began to talk rather freely about herself, it was obvious that she was preoccupied with death. She often said that she felt dead. She could recall only one time in her life when she had felt really alive. While reading in her ground-floor apartment one day, she heard a thump outside. She went to the window to investigate and saw a man lying in the yard with blood trickling from his mouth. He had just jumped from the roof of the building and died in a matter of seconds as she watched. The sight electrified her: "I came to life the moment I saw death."

Clearly, this gentle woman labored under a strong urge to kill, which had been satisfied for the moment by seeing the man die. The feeling that she was dead herself protected her against this urge. In childhood, she had been trained to repress her bad thoughts and feelings. When she discovered she could entertain the idea of killing, she tried to disown it, terrified at the thought she might yield to it. She was not aware that her mind wiped out these feelings; she simply knew that she felt out of things and not really alive. Thus, a sight that would horrify the average person vitalized her dramatically.

When a person reacts as this woman did in an encounter with death, it often signified that he has an enormous amount of aggression to discharge.

"When I feel like killing you, I kill my feelings instead"; this is the gist of the statements that patients, men and women, often make in treatment when they begin to understand how they cope with their hostility toward the people who are important to them. For example, an analyst's inadvertent remark to a patient in her forties about the fact that she was middle-aged made her furious, but she was quiet for a few minutes. Then she said, "If I had not blotted you out of my mind just now, I would have gotten off this couch and killed you." As a child, she had blotted out her mother in the same way during outbursts of rage. Similarly, patients' feelings that the analyst is not in the room with them often serve a protective function.

The reluctance of schizophrenic patients to express hostility tends to increase when they are exposed to sympathetic attitudes. On the other hand, when the analyst succeeds in communicating that he recognizes the patient's anxiety about behaving destructively in treatment, the patient is able to talk more spontaneously. It is impressive to observe the animated appearance of these patients after a session punctuated by angry verbal explosions. The periodic recurrence of these explosions after the patient has overcome his initial reluctance to disclose negative feelings suggests that internalized hatred builds up pressure that must be discharged from time to time. When these impulses are discharged in language, the symptoms of the illness tend to disappear.

These and other significant clues to the primary problem were found in the course of treatment of many schizophrenic patients. Considered singly, each observation contributed only a small piece of evidence; but together these clues formed a total picture of the illness.

The schizophrenic is a person who has placed himself in a psychological straightjacket to prevent himself from acting as his aggressive impulses tell him to act. Although he feels some love for others, his potential hatred is much greater, and he prefers to put himself out of commission psychologically rather than act on his strong aggressive impulses. Most likely he does not consciously recognize that he is sacrificing his own emotional health for the welfare of others. Nevertheless, he is at heart a socially minded human being who has developed a self-damaging way of controlling the destructive forces of his own mind to protect others. As long as this defense is successful, he is not a threat to society. Only when it fails does he engage in suicidal or homicidal behavior.

If the situation just depicted could not be altered, we would have an extremely difficult choice to make: to help the patient continue to internalize his hostility at the risk of destroying himself or to help him externalize it at the risk of destroying others. Fortunately, there is now a solution to this moral and psychological dilemma. The schizophrenic reaction is reversible. The patient can learn to discharge his hostile impulses without harming others, and language is a powerful tool for accomplishing this discharge.

Perhaps it should be explained at this point that an unloving mother is not the sole or primary cause of the schizophrenic reaction. Although schizophrenia is not an inherited condition, some people are predisposed to it by genetic or constitutional factors. Moreover, even when

the illness appears to originate in the mother-child relationship, the mother's attitude may not have been inappropriate. Whether she actually loved the infant, hated
him, or was indifferent to him is less significant than the
fact that the totality of his experience failed to meet his
specific emotional needs and caused him to perceive his
environment, on the whole, as an extremely frustrating
one. In any case, the child's emotional reality is that he
does not feel love. Let us assume that he correctly senses
that his mother does not love him; in this situation, the
healthy assumption is that she lacks the capacity to do so.
But the unloved child fights against admitting this to
himself. He would rather believe that he is undeserving of
his mother's love than that she is emotionally defective.
Thus, the desirable attitude is distorted in the child's
unconscious into the fiction that it is he who is defective
—i.e., a bad child who is undeserving of love. If he can just
stop hating, having bad thoughts, and misbehaving, he
can make himself over into the kind of child his mother
can love. In this way, he preserves the hope of receiving
love.

In the extreme form of schizophrenic withdrawal, the
patient regresses to a catatonic state in which early maternal figures who were incorporated into his psychic
structure (introjected objects) are warded off: that is, he
strives neither to love nor identify with them. For the
moment, the intensity of his destructive impulses
outweighs his libidinal impulses. But by using the available libidinal energy to immobilize himself, the catatonic
prevents destructive action and, because of the amount of
energy required to block action, is capable of only the most
rudimentary form of identification—imitation. This level

of incorporation apes the visual images of early infancy, actions to which no comprehensible meaning can be attached (Glover, 1949, p. 83).

We know that the ability to identify requires less cathexis than does loving. All that identification requires is the perception in the mind's object field of an auto-plastic representation, which can then be viewed as part of the self. Even less energy is needed for imitation. The catatonic's longing for love is present in the gestures with which he apes others. In his physical stereotypes, we see that the hallucinated objects of his longing, combined with his attacks, is frozen into his posturings. By aping (incorporating or swallowing) the gestures of his thera-pist, he simultaneously destroys his object. Since the psychic system has lost its ability to integrate impressions, this aping represents a simultaneous warding off and longing for the nurturing object. The barrier the catatonic erects by freezing his body mimics the sightless babe at the breast who makes his body rigid as he refuses the nipple. The bad nipple introject can only be rejected by a regres-sive stiffening of the body, and the catatonic has regressed to this primitive state.

NARCISSISM IN MANIC-DEPRESSIVE, PARANOID, AND PHOBIC REACTIONS

To describe the depressive reaction, Weiss (1963) modified the popular psychoanalytic theory that the ob-ject was swallowed because it was given up, and returned to an earlier theory that the object was first internalized at the infantile level through sensory impressions connected with gratifying experiences and, when given up, could not be shaken. "It clings like an echo," he wrote. This theoretical position helps the analyst understand patient communications such as, "There is a parasite or usurper inside me," when they are accompanied by self-attack.

Unlike the schizophrenic, the depressive patient seems to cling to the internalized transference figure with longing and hope while turning his attack against himself. He attacks his own worth to explain his deprivation. In his regression there may be some blurring of self-other images, which permits the self-attack to serve the function of object annihilation. The self-attack serves as a threat: If you mistreat me, I will punish you by depriving you of me. If you are like me, that will hurt you as much as your loss hurts me.

While the schizophrenic forgets his longings and obliterates his affects, the depressive maintains his resentment of internalized objects. He seems to hate his objects as an unshakable part of himself. Although he may be unable to relate with libido to the external person, he has enough energy to identify with the object impressions within from which he cannot shake loose. When the depressive person comes to treatment, he may say that he's worthless or hopeless or may portray himself as a disappointing person and insist that he should be thrown out of treatment. If he takes the paranoid position, he may be convinced that the analyst cannot stand him, but in either case, the patient attacks his own person by reacting with hopelessness, worthlessness, and helplessness. Paranoia and depression reflect the patient's confusion of self-impressions with object impressions. In paranoia self-impressions as well as object impressions are externalized and in depression object impressions are confused with the self. We sense that the depressive attacks the poisonous introject in an attempt to disown this "I" within that he wants to separate from his "real self." When he says, "I am worthless, I am hopeless," part of him is talking about the internalized other and trying to rid himself of it.

Schizophrenic and depressive patients, reliving those experiences that taught them how to destroy mind and self, present a preinterpretive problem. Paranoid patients struggle with feelings of helplessness and rage and generally, to avoid feeling humiliated and controlled, they project the self-deprecatory image onto a figure in the current environment. Weiss (1963) predicted that depressive patients with their self-accusatory style tended to become paranoid rather than manic, as predicted by early Freudian theory. Unlike the depressive who by attacking himself, attacks the person he has internalized and identified with, a paranoid patient may eject the hostile object onto the external environment. In both paranoia and melancholia, we see the withdrawal of libido from hallucinated wish-fulfilling objects re-created from the past.

In this pre-object period of weaker ego boundaries, it is a relatively small step for the person to eject the frustrating and critical portion of the object, which is experienced as an intruder into his psyche, by perceiving the introject as external to his ego. Weiss related the paranoid fear of being poisoned by the external object to the deep fear of reincorporating the bad image and deeper desire to let it back in. He reported that regressed paranoid patients were afraid they would succumb to the deeper wish to reincorporate the object. When these patients were not protecting themselves from bad food or other substances that penetrate the body, or from sexual advances, they heard voices telling them what to do. In fact, voices may reoccupy the body. During a reintegration with the externalized part of the self, several patients described their minds as filled with invisible people who "are not me."

When the paranoid patient's mind is occupied in this way, the patient struggles with helpless rage and feels that matters are beyond his control. However, he is less humiliated by this "occupation" than he would be by being helpless with others in the real world.

In hypomania, the patient may perceive others as bad and, in the role of conquering hero, take "justifiable" aggressive action. Thus the destructive impulses of infancy are projected allowing the self to remain identified with the critical object. By perceiving the bad self as being in the environment and by using aggressive impulses in an attack against the environment, the hypomanic maintains comfortable feelings about himself. If the manic can successfully sublimate his rage by becoming a fighter for causes, he can vent his wrath against external evils in a socially useful way. When an individual is able to channel his destructive urges into socially acceptable attacks on external situations, bad images no longer remain in the ego field of his mind. Instead the critical object has been internalized. The self is not under attack from inside, as in depression, or from outside, as in some cases of paranoia. Destructive actions become possible as justifiable punishment for projected misdeeds.

Within the limits of this chapter, it would be difficult to do justice to the wide range of pathologies that can be understood as adaptations to the tension created by the patterns of frustration during the early months of life. In depersonalization, the patient gives up certain aspects of the self. Behind his conscious fear of loving, we may find rage about remembered deprivation, fear of destructive impulses, and fear of losing himself in regression. Anorexia and other somatic conditions remind us that the avenues of discharge available to the infant during early tension-producing, prefeeling states are limited.

CONCLUSION

The object field of the mind is a fantasy area in which a patient may perceive the bad or depriving images as alien from the self. In psychosis, the patient banishes the object image from his mind or confuses it with the self so that one or the other can be externalized.

A number of patterns of self-attack are difficult to treat by traditional analytic techniques, and it is in relation to treatment of these patterns that modern analysis is making significant inroads. When a person gives up his narcissistic defense, he may engage in self-destructive acts such as suicide or self-mutilation, or resort to homicide. The narcissistic defense breaks down when the amount of libidinal cathexis is insufficient to balance the aggressive drive. When the narcissistic defense fails and the aggression is turned against the environment, psychotic eruption is avoided if the patient can annihilate the memory image and related feelings by the process of externalizing to a current figure in the environment. Whereas classical psychoanalysts linked these diagnostic categories with libido and repression of oedipal wishes, e.g., paranoia with libido (or, more specifically, with sexual inversion), modern psychoanalysts seek the psychic constructs that successfully resolve these patterns of self-attack, and accept as valid only those constructs that do resolve the self-attack.

No one theory is adequate to explain the behavior of all our patients. From the emotional experiences we share with a particular patient grows the theoretical awareness of that patient's life history. The energy constructs described here have been extremely helpful in understanding the infant's and the regressed adult's reactions to object impressions. As the ego develops, energy is used to integrate aural and visual impressions echoed within the mental structure. Sorting non-ego from ego and reality from internal impressions requires a quantum of energy that is not available when tied up in warding off visual impressions. This theory of internalization and externalization of early visual images conceptualizes the dynamics of the severe narcissistic disorders in economic terms. If the individual case determines the best theory to explain it, we must ask: what are the advantages of developing theories to explain the psychic structure of our patients? In our work with patients, we find that as we begin to understand the patient's disguised communications, he is freed to develop his own understanding of his emotional life. Although our patients' understanding may be different from ours and our solutions may not be those they would choose, they seem to need our efforts and understanding. When their understanding is correct for them, they are able to change.

THE NARCISSISTIC
TRANSFERENCE

THROUGH ITS CONCERN with the development of therapeutic responses to narcissistic patterns, modern psychoanalysis has opened the field of psychoanalysis to research and investigation into genetic, constitutional, and early environmental factors in personality development. But to develop a therapeutic response to the preverbal patient, it was necessary to explore what it meant to hide behind the narcissistic defense.

The narcissistic personality was poorly understood when these investigations began. The traditional view that the patient must have a sufficiently mature ego with which the analyst can establish a working alliance was abandoned when modern analysts became interested in studying persons with preoedipal, preverbal disorders to determine how they can be treated and their illnesses reversed.

Much of the modern analyst's time and attention has been devoted to the methods of treating narcissim. To call modern psychoanalysis a new approach to narcissism seems fitting because it is in this area that the discipline has made its major contributions to the body of knowledge known as psychoanalysis. Working with individuals with fixations in the first year or two of life has led to the finding that although these cases do not always respond satisfactorily to work with early emotional defenses, new techniques can yield impressive results.

The idea was new that analytic treatment of the preverbal patient could be based on Freud's concepts of transference and resistance and that, through transference, the patient could re-experience the traumas of the first two years of life as well as later verbal conflicts. Although traditional analysis had proved successful with the hysterias, the phobias, and the compulsions, Freud was unable to modify the interpretive approach to suit the treatment of narcissistic disorders. Despite the numerous clues he gave his colleagues in his dreams and other disguised communications, he never understood his own preoedipal wishes. As a result, he was unable to deal with the feelings induced in him by paranoid or schizophrenic patients or by other oral personalities.

THE NARCISSISTIC DEFENSE

The analyst resolves the adult patient's repetitive self-attacks by changing the flow of destructive impulsivity. When the patient is frustrated, the appropriate way to discharge his feelings is to put them into words. If he is prevented from doing so when frustrated and feeling deprived by the analyst, he usually bottles up the aggression: in other words, he turns these feelings inward and begins to attack the self. *This is referred to as the narcis-sistic defense.*

To explain the patient's need to resort to the narcissistic defense, we think of the interpersonal patterns that created pre-ego, prefeeling patterns of discharge. In a regression to this emotional level of development predating language, the patient's communications return to the timeless world of infancy with its lack of temporal and spatial continuity and the inability to predict or anticipate events. When regressed, the narcissistic person does not seem able to distinguish between inner and outer reality. In the words of one patient who got in touch with this process: "I want to kill you to get you out of my head."

The analyst tries to keep in mind that when the patient brings the narcissistic defense into the transference relationship, he is doing it to protect the analyst from his hostility, as he did the mothering figure, by attacking himself. When a patient tells an analyst that the failures in the analysis are his own fault, not the analyst's, the analyst attempts to redirect the patient's self-attacks and the inward flow of destructivity if possible. If the analyst provides the proper environment, the patient will re-experience emotional reactions in his relationship with the analyst that resemble those he had at some point in the past when his maturation was blocked. To prevent motor discharge when old destructive impulses are aroused in the treatment, each patient returns to his own early adaptive modes, which in the context of the present situation may appear irrational. If the patient can relive that period with the analyst-that is, develop a transference-the analyst may be able to make the appropriate communications that will free the patient to mature.

The patient who is treated while regressed to the first

years of life develops a narcissistic transference rather than an object transference. But analysts ask: "Do we want a narcissistic transference to develop?" We do because in a negative, regressed state, the patient may experience the analyst as being like him or part of him. Or the analyst may not exist for him. The syntonic feeling of oneness is a curative one, while the feeling of aloneness, the withdrawn state, is merely protective. Because traces of narcissism remain in everyone, we seek, when beginning treatment, to create an environment that will facilitate a narcissistic transference so that, first, we can work through the patient's narcissistic aggression. The extent to which the patient wards us off and avoids emotional contact tells us the degree to which he is narcissistically fixated. He will gradually increase his contacts with us if we create the appropriate environment. To establish the ego-syntonic atmosphere in which the patient can view us as being like him, or at least as non-threatening and nonjudgmental, modern analysts carefully avoid exposing the patient to any uninvited communication or interpretation. When the patient feels that he can say and feel things without taking action, his emotional contacts with the analyst will increase. Bringing out whatever narcissism remains in the personality helps the person who has a minimum amount of narcissistic defensiveness to remain in treatment when his impulsiveness surfaces. By not providing the patient with excessive communication, the analyst can maintain the ego-syntonic environment necessary to master his patient's destructive impulses.

Unfortunately, it is difficult for the analyst to remain objective when the patient expresses a narcissistic transference, or attacks unceasingly the analyst's faults and perceptively pinpoints the sensitive spots in his personality and treatment methods. If the patient announces that he is destroying himself, has done terrible things to himself, and is not finished being self-destructive, the analyst's defenses are usually aroused against induced feelings of hopelessness, isolation, or rage. It is easier to put distance between himself and this unpleasant, provocative patient by thinking, "Poor fellow, he needs my help. Perhaps I should be supportive or gratifying to the patient." But this approach leads the patient to attack himself even more and increases the analyst's feeling of hopelessness.

NARCISSISM IN A PHOBIC CASE

The following case, reported by Meadow, revealed a pattern in which a patient who had lived most of her life behind the manic defense, developed a thin disguise for her narcissism in phobic symptomatology. Barbara presented an interesting combination of phobias and hypomanic defenses used to deal with intolerance of negative affects. Using the manic defense, this patient externalized her badness and was able to turn her destructive impulses against the environment. This enabled her to maintain a relatively comfortable internal state.

Barbara worked as an executive in a large male-dominated firm and devoted enormous amounts of energy to the fight for women's rights. These efforts kept her relatively symptom-free for years. Later, she was an active crusader against injustice. These crusades were a further attempt at stabilization. Eventually, however, because these activities did not satisfy her desire for revenge against the original parent figures, Barbara became more concerned with the evil around her. Her need to distort events into black and white issues demonstrated an intensification of the split between the bad self and the good object. Previous therapy had not successfully integrated these good and bad images and the split had occurred when her former therapist, appearing unethical to Barbara, necessitated further defensive measures.

Between the time her first treatment ended and the second began, Barbara's phobic symptomatology appeared. The phobias served to limit her social contacts and apparently protected her from a desire to act on her destructive impulses. The price she paid was to remain in suspended animation and a double bind. Her longing to be close to others and to be with a much admired person aroused fears that she would lose the protective barrier against past feelings and led to the symptom of agoraphobia, which kept her reclusive. When she did allow herself to enter a personal relationship, she experienced a strong desire to get away from the person and be liberated from the tie for fear she would act on her negative feelings. This resulted in the symptom of claustrophobia.

Barbara considered herself to be an independent woman and felt disdain for her female friends who tolerated unhappy marriages. She would rather be free to enjoy herself than be married; she could sleep as long as she wished, soak in a warm tub as long as she wanted, and have sexual relations when and with whom she wanted, according to her mood. She did not have to "submit" as her married women friends did, and best of all, she could avoid the constant bickering that her married friends considered normal. She also enjoyed being free to go wherever and whenever she pleased.

This patient could not tolerate tight fitting clothing.

She had difficulty finding dresses that were bearable; belts were an impossible restriction. She preferred the kind of dress that one can forget about.

In a group, Barbara usually felt tense—as if everyone was "on top of her." Although she did not like to ride in a car too long with another person, long drives alone were tolerable. When she entered treatment for the second time, one of her presenting symptoms was a fear of elevators. The analyst's first impression was that she was suffering from a phobic reaction—that her symptoms served to ward off feelings of helplessness and dependency—and her basic struggle was to rid herself of attachments that created these feelings. Her history revealed that the desire to rid herself of longings was in the service of object protection. Her claustrophobia, panic about tight-fitting clothing, and fear of small crowded rooms, elevators, and the intensity of marital relations protected her from the narcissistic defense as it is manifested in schizophrenia. She wanted to be free, but the message of her agoraphobia was "I do not want the freedom that I consciously crave; I *want* to be tied to people, but I cannot tolerate the feelings."

Analysts have written extensively about the oedipal conflicts expressed in the phobia, so these conflicts will not be detailed here. In fact, these conflicts were not significant in Barbara's case. Fear of circumscribed events and objects (the phobic reaction), provided adequate protection against total emotional withdrawal, allowing some fluctuations and conflict. A modern psychoanalyst would not attempt to disrupt this defense until the underlying aggression could be discharged sufficiently.

The removal of Barbara's phobias at the point described here could predictably lead to a more severe regression. Treatment in such cases entails the development of a narcissistic transference in which the patient can be presented with a faithful twin image.

As treatment progressed, Barbara continued to present her fears. She was concerned with her fear of enclosed and open spaces. Her phobias served precisely the same function that withdrawal serves, but they allowed her to preserve the perceptual and cognitive functions. Rage, not sexuality, was to be avoided. So long as the therapist kept her distance, Barbara did not fear the couch, and by focusing on the content of her phobias and her life, she avoided real closeness during the sessions. When she was tottering on the narrow divide between her fear of closed and open spaces, what surfaced in the session was that being liberated meant freedom from the feelings that relationships aroused in her, and particularly the feeling of helpless rage. In the transference, she revealed her desire to annihilate anyone who aroused in her longings for emotional closeness. Longings made her feel weak, inadequate and helpless. The phobic anxiety was a reaction to reemerging feelings. But loss of closeness aroused the counter phobia that she would find herself in an objectless world; at that point, she wanted to return to closed-in places and to some contact with people. The claustrophobic response appeared when people were overstimulating. Clearly, Barbara was symbolically asking: "Should I enter human relations, get involved, and suffer all the pain of hostile feelings, or should I keep myself safe?"

Barbara arranged her social life so that her male friends appeared on demand. She had a list of three or four current boyfriends, and when she wanted a sexual relationship, she telephoned one of them.

On the oedipal level, Barbara's sexual arrangements and fear of her sexuality can be considered a compromise, but we are concerned here with the nurturing conflict. Barbara was drawn to a potentially nurturing situation, but she protected herself from it by demeaning the object. The men in her life served two purposes: providing intimate relationships without intimacy and the freedom to back off when closeness threatened. In other words, these men provided partial relationships. Barbara thought of all people, male and female, as mother figures: i.e., her relationships were preoedipal. The phobias served to provide her with controlled mothering that was similar to the infant's desire to have its mother on call to provide services. The phobia's deepest disguised message, however, was infantile longing and the wish to destroy or incorporate the object as it was perceived during Barbara's first year of life.

Barbara's first adjustment was a mania that worked for her. Later she created phobias that also worked. The symbiotic struggle between self and introject is seen in alternating states of claustrophobia and agoraphobia in which the fear of losing the needed images oscillated with the wish to destroy the unsatisfying image. When her fear of destructive impulses dominated, Barbara became claustrophobic. This type of patient may consciously experience an internal restriction (the counterforce) on the somatic level and express thoughts of the wish for unrestricted freedom.

Phobias are common enough symptoms in mental hospitals, where we find patients who rip off their clothes or are unable to leave a room or a particular area. These symptoms often appear as part of the schizophrenic picture.

In cases such as Barbara's, the determining factor in the symptomatology and how the patient will play out his interpersonal relations is a result of the way he visualizes the early maternal environment and his feelings about the quality of mothering he received. As he learns to give up old pathways of discharge and differentiate between the self and other, he discovers the rewards of personal relationships.

CONCLUSION

The psyche of the preverbal patient contains a strong libidinal attachment to others and a strong desire for the warmth and closeness that others can provide. This is the kind of closeness one expects during the first year of life– to be held, to be walked, to be rocked, to be talked to, and in general to be soothed. It is these longings that are reactivated in the narcissistic transference. In fact, these longings help the patient decide to protect the significant persons in his life. When he becomes murderously enraged, because of frustration, all that stands between him and his impulses are his libidinal feelings for his mother. In the treatment relationship, the analyst eventually becomes the person with whom the patient must work out and resolve his emotional problems. Of course, every patient hopes that the analyst will eventually provide the gratification he seeks. But, as analysts, we are interested in training the patient to seek gratification outside the analysis.

The modern analytic view is that the mature personality can experience frustration and object hatred without the necessity of destroying either itself or the other person. In regression, pathways established in infancy may be reactivated when the object does not provide the needed tension-reducing gratification. Thus, the available supply of libido is tied up in the defensive functions of object protection, in the denial of feeling that results, and in attempts to control destructive impulsiveness. When these views are applied to the garbled communications of patients, the messages become clearer. We see the attack on the patients' secondary mental processes when they report their confused states of mind, distort external reality to ward off impressions, and withdraw cathexis from the external world. When frustrated, patients resort to increasingly pathological retreats from their destructive impulsiveness to maintain a tolerable level of tension.

When the patient experiences frustration in the transference, his need to protect those he loves is eventually brought into the transference. Typically, the narcissistic personality chooses to attack a part of itself.

In treating narcissism we have found that patients develop a narcissistic transference in which, to protect the analyst, they turn destructive impulsiveness against the self. The analyst is then confronted with the task of resolving the patient's repetitive self attacks. To analyze the narcissistic resolution of conflict, it is helpful to view the self-destructive reactions as organized responses in which the flow of libidinal and aggressive energy can be understood by studying the organism's early attempts to master tension.

THE NARCISSISTIC COUNTERTRANSFERENCE:

A Theory of Emotional Contagion and the Toxoid Response

IF HUMAN BEINGS are capable of influencing each other's emotional states, and emotional states influence human behavior, then the factor of emotional induction becomes an important one for scientific consideration.

Emotions are of considerable significance for the functioning of the individual. Each one of us is aware of the fact that behavior we feel impelled to perform is so much easier to carry out than behavior in which we do not wish to engage. Emotions facilitate behavior compatible with the same emotions. Their relative absence may make behavior a great effort. Therefore, for the spontaneously well-functioning human being, it is necessary that there be available at all times a supply of emotions that will facilitate behavior leading to a good adjustment to the immediate reality situation. It is then that conditions are favorable for the individual to be spontaneously well-functioning and well-adjusted.

The fact that emotions can be induced is highly significant because if the proper emotion facilitates proper behavior, then a considerable part of psychiatric therapy and re-education might well be directed to the induction in human beings of the kind of emotions they lack in order to produce a satisfactory adjustment.

In the sphere of biological medicine, there is nothing equivocal about the meaning of contagion—it denotes the process by which disease is transmitted from person to person, whether directly or indirectly. Over the centuries, the annals of medical science have recorded man's efforts to identify and wipe out the forces implicated in the spread of the various contagious disorders.

Although the spread of emotion is a less threatening notion, emotional contagion is more likely to be coupled with the transmission of harmful rather than healthful influences. In the past, emotional contagion was linked with the black arts of witchcraft; in our age, the phenomenon is primarily associated with the spread of antisocial attitudes, disordered behavior, and mental illnesses.

In the early literature of psychiatry, many references to emotional or mental contagion are found in case reports of induced, communicated, or imposed insanity. The majority of these cases involve the development of similar psychotic reactions, frequently delusions of persecution, in persons who have been in long and intimate contact, usually members of the same family. More often than not, it has been found that a relatively submissive and dependent child, sibling, or spouse was "contaged" by a more dominant family member suffering from paranoid schizophrenia or paranoia. A French psychiatrist who hospitalized such a family pair in 1860 called the condition *folie à deux*—double madness or insanity in two's. Flournay reported a case in the Swiss Archives of Neurology and Psychiatry (1927), involving a middle-aged woman who persuaded her teenage half-brother to believe her delusive idea that her former employer would destroy both of them if they opened the door or shutters of their home. This internment did not end until the woman realized that the boy was on the verge of death from hunger and cold. It was observed that he lacked the intense emotional tone of an authentic delusion, and his condition was characterized as "no more than a particular case of general suggestibility." Like others so infected, the boy recovered quickly under treatment.

Observation of infants has yielded ideas on emotional contagion. Based on her work with infants in the late forties and early fifties, Escalona (1953), a psychoanalytically-trained researcher interested in emotional development during the early months of life, reported her impression that long before speech or gestures play a role in the relationship between the mother and her infant, they transmit their feelings, purposes, and intentions through two distinctly different ways: communication and contagion. Escalona reserved the term communication for the conscious and purposeful sending and receiving of information. This is, of course, wholly nonverbal on the baby's part, although the mother may verbalize information "at least in the form of thought." Transmission of a feeling state through contagion is, on the other hand, "never fully subject to voluntary control by the person from whom it emanates." Both kinds of transmission may be onesided or they may be mutual; in the latter case, something flows from mother to baby and back again. Escalona compared the one-way communication to listening to the radio; and the two-way transmission to conversation on the telephone.

Contagion, in the words of Escalona, refers to

Those processes whereby a feeling state transmits itself from mother to baby, as when an infant cries when held by an acutely tense and anxious person but seems quite content when held by one who is relaxed: or when a baby cries but then settles down merely upon being spoken to and patted in a reassuring manner. . . . An excited, worried mother may try to convey reassurance, but the baby, if he is susceptible to contagion, will respond to her actual feeling state. On the other hand, a person who really feels calm can, if she is skillful, intentionally convey a sense of calmness to the baby [1953].

Such social interactions constitute the most fascinating and mysterious aspects of infancy research to Escalona, and she added, "I would give much to know just what it is that flows from the reassurer to the reassured, and by what path-ways." Escalona (1974) wrote:

Since that time a good deal has been learned about the "pathways" through which currents of feeling and specific messages are transmitted from one person to another. The microanalysis of behavior (i.e. Birdwhistell and many others) has delineated consistent patterns in subtle nuances of postural, gestural, muscular and temporal aspects of non-verbal behavior which express tension states, aversions, preferences, and much else. With schizophrenic patients in particular, it has been demonstrated that some patients typically receive from their mothers simultaneous but contradictory messages; one in words and consciously intended, the other in 'body language' and expressive of unconscious or at least unacknowledged wishes and intentions on the mother's part. Non-verbal contagion and communication are almost certainly part and parcel of everyday social interactions in the normal realm as well as in pathology.

Watching so much for contagion between infants and mothers made Escalona aware that it also operates significantly in adult relations. In her view, currents of feeling are spread by contagion and operate significantly between therapists and patients, between lovers, in such ordinary situations as entering a store and then leaving it because one does not like the atmosphere, in choosing to remain with one group rather than another at a cocktail party, or in becoming uncomfortable when sitting next to people who are angry with one another even though they do not reveal their anger through words or action.

Some disturbed children are particularly susceptible to emotional contagion, and they may be very much aware of their tendencies to be overrun by the feelings of others. A twelve-year-old girl with a tendency toward anxiety and depression remarked to a psychiatric social worker in a matter-of-fact way, "I caught my fear of mice from my big sister."

A highly narcissistic adolescent boy often had great difficulty distinguishing his own feelings from those of the people with whom he associated. He frequently operated in terms of their feelings, and had little awareness of his own. In treatment he demonstrated great facility for picking up certain feelings that were never directly communicated to him. In the early stages of treatment, severely disturbed children usually operate very much more in tune with the therapist's feelings than with their own.

In family therapy, many children pick up the feelings of parents and describe them with amazing accuracy. In the presence of the children, the parents frequently deny harboring the feeling, but they may own up to it after the child has left the room. In many instances they have been trying to conceal feelings of hatred for one another.

A mother who feels hatred for the father tends to carry over the same attitude to the child and act it out with him even though she feels great love for the child. The child, under the influence of this non-verbalized hatred, behaves very negativistically. The phenomena is encountered repeatedly—a Medea complex. No less than the mother who hates or is indifferent to her child, a basically loving mother can create severe psychological damage in a child who is hypersensitive to her hatred for his father.

We have acquired a great deal of knowledge about the existence of emotional contagion in psychoanalysis, but this knowledge relates primarily to the existence of emotional contagion of patients undergoing treatment together and its negative and positive values for them. But practically nothing has been written about the harnessing of the contagious forces by the psychoanalyst. In other words, handling countertransference feelings is not taken into consideration in planning and conducting the psychoanalysis. One crucial issue is this: should the analyst deliberately expose himself to emotional contagion? Should he open himself up to experiencing the feelings and impulses of his patients and if so, how should he utilize them to help the patients achieve their goals in treatment?

Freud solved the problem, theoretically, by formulating the concept of transference. That is, the feelings that the patient develops and communicates during the course of his communications on the analytic couch are transferred to the analyst from parents and other emotionally significant persons in the patient's life. Freud also gave heed to the feelings that arise in the analyst as a result of the patient's emotional influence, and stressed the necessity of recognizing and overcoming the phenomena, to which he gave the name countertransference.

In a letter written to Binswanger (1913), Freud refers to countertransference as one of the most difficult problems in psychoanalysis. His concern with the misuse of countertransference feelings is expressed in the letter.

> What is given to the patient should indeed never be a spontaneous affect, but always consciously allotted, and then more or less of it as the need may arise. Occasionally a great deal [is given], but never from one's own unconscious. This I should regard as the formula. In other words, one must always recognize one's countertransference and rise above it, only then is one free oneself. To give someone too little because one loves him too much is being unjust to the patient and a technical error [p. 50].

When Freud warned his colleagues of the dangers of countertransference, he may have been thinking about the celebrated case of Anna O. This interesting woman, who coined the phrase "talking cure," was treated by Josef Breuer, a senior colleague and friend of Freud, and the co-developer of the psychoanalytic method. Anna O. apparently induced her own feelings in Breuer and these became fused with his own emotions. Breuer's wife became jealous of this attractive young woman to whom her husband was devoting so much time and thought, and one day Breuer, in a state of anger, abandoned the patient, only to be summoned back to her home a few hours later. He found her in the throes of pseudocyesis, a fantasy of childbirth. He calmed her down with hypnosis and then went off with his wife on a second honeymoon. Anna O.

suffered a series of relapses before recovering, and Breuer left psychotherapy vowing never to go through such an ordeal again.

The exclusion of any reference to negative feelings induced by the analysand is characteristic of Freud. In another letter to Binswanger, he referred to a patient who "actually has been running away from me, since I was able to tell her the real secret of her illness (revengeful and murderous impulses against her husband)." He then dismisses the woman in these words: "analytically unfit for anyone" [p. 62]. If Freud ever confronted this patient or any others with feelings of hatred, he appears not to have done so through the "consciously allotted" affects that he had already advocated for conveying feelings of love. This may help to explain his pessimistic views about the treatment of narcissistic disorders. But, "apart from Freud's failure to address himself to the induced feelings of hatred, his statement on countertransference is entirely compatible with the modern psychoanalytic approach to the deeply narcissistic person" (Spotnitz, 1963).

The training procedures that have developed since the early years of psychoanalysis are calculated to prevent a replay of the Anna O. and Breuer episode. One aspect of training is a personal analysis of the future practitioner. Supervision, the practice of conducting the first cases with the aid of an experienced analyst, is another aspect of training. Many candidates in the process of training are indoctrinated with the idea that it is important to maintain a neutral attitude, to suppress and repress feelings, and to prevent oneself from communicating feelings to the patient. Analysts who teach this approach are maintaining the so-called blank screen attitude as a matter of preference and are conducting treatment primarily as an intellectual endeavor. In brief, the tradition in conducting psychoanalysis offers little encouragement to the idea of exposing oneself to emotional contagion.

Many of the early departures from the attitude of emotional detachment were accidental variations that were only reported when they led to desirable consequences. More analysts today are willing to have the feelings, but a great deal of confusion exists both on the specific values of opening up to a patient's feelings, and on the question of timing and the desirability of making such reactions known to the patient.

Most analysts remember that emotional detachment has been one of the cornerstones in the structure of psychoanalysis and that Freud (1912), in his essays on technique, warned repeatedly against any kind of emotional involvement with patients. He went so far as to urge analytic therapists to take as their model "the surgeon who puts aside his own feelings, including that of human sympathy, and concentrates his mind on one single purpose, that of performing the operation as skillfully as possible." To elaborate on this analogy: just as the surgeon must avoid contamination from the pus draining from his patient's incision, the therapist must avoid becoming immersed in a *folie à deux* or *folie à beaucoup*.

Some of the difficulties in learning to utilize contagious feelings must be attributed to the fact that the real emotions induced in the analyst by the patient have not been adequately differentiated from the reactions that are based on the analyst's own adjustment patterns. Contact with the patient stimulates both types of reactions—that is, reactions based on objective observation of the patient as a real person (objective countertransference) and the arousal of feelings that the analyst has developed for significant figures in his own life (subjective counter-transference). His own training analysis is oriented to helping him recognize the subjective countertransference feelings and to counteract the tendency to attach them to patients. The intrusion of these subjective reactions into the treatment relationship is always undesirable. It is these reactions in the analyst that are usually focused on in professional discussions of countertransference. To relate to a patient in terms of the analyst's own adjustment to persons in his own emotional life history is to use the treatment relationship as an outlet for personal emotional gratification.

We distinguish these feelings from the emotions realistically induced in the analyst by objective observation of the patient since the latter provide the analyst with a valuable tool for understanding the early emotional relations of his patient.

To clarify the difference between these reactions, let us suggest an analogous optical phenomenon. Any person with normal vision who closes his eyes after looking at a red light will see a green after-image. But for a person whose vision is abnormal, the after-image may be grey or some other color, depending on the nature and extent of his impairment. Just as the green and grey images are aroused by the same light, the objective and subjective countertransference reactions are both aroused by the patients. But, whereas subjective countertransference is altered in some way by atypical tendencies in the analyst, objective countertransference is the predictable response of the emotionally mature observer. The latter is what we have in mind when we refer to the possibility of exploiting emotional contagion for therapeutic purposes (Spotnitz, 1969b, p. 163).

THE THERAPEUTIC USE
OF EMOTIONAL CONTAGION

Probably the most widespread use of the induced emotions is as an aid in understanding the patient—understanding that encompasses both the origin and nature of the problem that brought him into treatment and his immediate behavior. In short, the analyst who permits himself to experience the feelings transmitted by the patient can derive information from them that the patient is not providing verbally. In recent years, it has been noted that induced feelings can contribute to the diagnostic fact-finding process and to the understanding of specific problems that arise in treatment. Kernberg (1965) and Kohut (1971) have written on the phenomena of narcissistic identification of the analyst with the analysand. A passive attitude is maintained so long as the patient remains narcissistically self-absorbed or is functioning cooperatively. Direct attempts to elicit some personal information about the analyst or to involve the analyst in some emotional problem that the patient is unable to express in words may, if the origins are understood, be "returned" to the patient by the analyst through a response that reflects the pattern of the patient's resistance. Verbal injections of the emotions that he has transmitted to the analyst are fed back to the patient in graduated doses to reduce his disposition to future upheavals. To understand the patient's attempts at contact, the analyst has to experience his feelings. When the patient feels them as belonging to the analyst (an externalization combined with recognition), he is able to think about them and to discharge them as his own in mature language.

Since this process is similar to immunizing the body against a particular antigen, such as that of diphtheria, by destroying its toxicity but leaving it capable of inducing the formation of antibodies, this use of feeding back induced emotions in carefully timed and graduated doses is *referred to as a toxoid response* (Spotnitz, 1963). Exploiting the phenomena of mutual contagion helps the analyst experience the patient's feelings; after he understands how they originated, he returns them to the patient in a highly specific way to help him discharge his feelings in language. If the patient proves indifferent or over-stimulated, the emotional confrontation is discontinued. It is continued if it produces new understanding or ideas the patient was unable to discuss previously, that is, so long as he engages in progressive communication. Identification with an emotionally responsive analyst helps the patient feel and verbalize destructive impulses that have been warded off. When the patient can do this the toxic quality gradually diminishes.

Spotnitz (1969) commented as follows on the concept of objective countertransference:

> While the patient develops a transference, the analyst usually develops a countertransference which is based on unconscious reactions to the patient's transference attitudes and behavior. The success of the therapy depends in large measure upon the analyst's ability to feel the tendencies toward instinctual discharge. The capacity to sense the latent emotions and to help the patient feel them determines whether the relationship is grounded in genuine emotional understanding, or is primarily an intellec-

tual exercise. An essential capacity for an analyst is the capacity to feel induced emotions; to help the patient to verbalize them is the process of resolving his resistances (Unpubl.).

A few analysts have reported instances in which the expression of negative feelings that were induced in them by patients actually proved helpful to these patients and triggered progress in their treatment. For example, Franz Alexander (1961) ended an apparent stalemate in one case by admitting to his patient that he disliked him.

Emotional responses figured prominently in the resolution of the resistances of the highly narcissistic young man called Fred (Spotnitz, 1963). Directly or indirectly, during the early stages of his treatment, he would start to verbalize thoughts about getting off the couch to attack his analyst and then quickly lapse into silence. Interventions at the time were designed to help him talk about his destructive impulses and to tame them somewhat through such release. Feelings of guilt about what he might say clammed him up. He also had strong fears that talking about his impulses would force him to act on them. He was convinced that his destructive urges proved that he was incurable.

The repetitive quality of his threats aroused a good deal of resentment in the analyst; even more was aroused by Fred's insistence that his disturbing feelings and fantasied acts of primitive violence made him unique. He fought strenuously against the notion that such impulses were natural and that an important aspect of one's rearing was to learn to direct them.

It occurred to the analyst that the way to solve this problem was to demonstrate to the patient that the analyst had similar thoughts and feelings about him. First attempts to convey this idea were ineffectual. "Don't try that stuff," the patient said when one of his threats was turned back at him. "You're repeating what I say, but you don't really mean it." But the analyst had the impression that he was unconsciously egging him on. The analyst bided his time until the feelings induced in him by the patient's outbursts of rage permitted him to respond with equal vehemence.

Fred appeared to be ready for such a response when he shouted in a moment of fury: "I'll bash your head in." "No you won't," the analyst exploded back at him, "because I'll bash yours in before you can get off the couch." Though Fred felt no need to defend himself against attack, he responded to this expression of genuine feeling by exclaiming: "You really do hate me as much as I hate you, and you can be even more vicious!"

Fred gained relief and security from the analyst's emotional responses. As his terror of speaking of destructive urges gradually diminished, they lost their toxic quality. If someone he respected and relied on could accept such urges and verbalize them, so could he. When he permitted himself voluntarily to dwell on long-outlawed feelings and thoughts of violence and found that he could do so without acting impulsively, the toxoid responses were discontinued.

As positive feelings for his own ego mounted, Fred matured sufficiently to accept, either spontaneously or with the aid of interpretation, many libidinal as well as aggressive impulses that had been ego-alien. By this time, the induced feelings that the analyst had stored up for long periods during the first two years of the case were rarely employed as a therapeutic instrument. Interpretations tend to dissipate these feelings; but no effort was made to sustain them when the interpretations were acceptable to his ego (Spotnitz and Nagelberg, 1960).

In work with seriously disturbed children and adults, it is important to utilize the feelings induced by the patient when formulating interpretations or questions. The induced feelings may be returned to the patient in a reflection of the patient's resistance. This helps make the patient more aware of what he is experiencing at the moment, and helps him to verbalize these intrapsychic experiences in a progressive way. When the emotional response is timed to the patient's contact function in his attempts to directly involve the analyst, uncontrollable reactions may be prevented. In analytic terms, this is the method used to resolve resistance.

Highly narcissistic patients often get bogged down in repeating the same idea over and over again; they sound like a phonograph record going around and around in the same groove. The type of objective interpretation that a less disturbed person usually responds to is rarely effective in resolving a so-called narcissistic resistance. More helpful than an intellectual explanation of why they are repeating the same communication is some intervention based on the feelings that the patient's repetitive communication is inducing in the analyst. (A case study in this volume [p. 176] demonstrates the use of induced states to resolve a narcissistic transference resistance.) Usually, the use of induced feelings in this way helps the patient get back on the track of progressive communication again. To express this in technical language, the resistance is temporarily resolved. The patient will continue to revert to the same resistance pattern over and over again until he succeeds in mastering the resistant behavior and giving it up—in other words, working it through.

The toxoid response is created from the feelings induced in the analyst. To provide a gravely narcissistic person with treated doses of the toxoid responses he experienced in childhood, and re-experiences in the transference, facilitates the release of the intense emotions he has bottled up. However, the very fact that the emotional quality of the transference reactions is thereby intensified introduces the possibility of a new source of error: contamination of the analytic situation by an inappropriate emotional communication (Spotnitz et al., 1956). This can be more damaging than an incorrect interpretation. Transference reactions are dampened by the neutral attitude of the analyst who limits himself to the classical approach. The treatment edition of the patient's nuclear conflict is weaker, so that wrong interpretations are of relatively little significance. They do not create reactions in the patient that are likely to distort or change the toxic emotions of the transference neurosis (Spotnitz, 1963, p. 621).

The use of induced feelings makes an important contribution to the working-through process in the treatment of the schizophrenic and other patients whose problems originated in the preverbal period of life. The analyst becomes aware of the toxic emotions that interfered with this person's maturation and functioning in life. In helping the patient discharge these toxic emotions in language, the analyst also recognizes that the defensive and repressive operations through which the patient held these emotions in check are in the process of dissolution. The patient induces similar or antithetical states in the analyst, and if the analyst can tolerate them indefinitely without acting on them, he can utilize them to neutralize the pathological effects of the patient's past experiences. Preverbal resistances are often upheld by maturational needs that are not being met by life experience, and the analyst has to engage in an emotional communication to resolve these resistances. The reason for employing the induced emotions in this manner is that it helps the patient to outgrow his resistance.

The residue of undifferentiated feelings that a schizophrenic patient in a state of narcissistic transference induces in the analyst provides many clues to the nature of his emotional relationship with his mother during the first two years of life. For example, a person who experienced a great deal of emotional deprivation in infancy, may in a treatment situation when he is bottling up rage, induce feelings of indifference or unrelatedness in the analyst. The analyst may feel impatience or contempt when the patient bogs down in complaints. The sorting out of the induced feelings is engaged in to help the patient understand the psychic events of his infancy.

Some of the feelings that are induced by the personality and behavior of a severely disturbed patient are those that the patient presumably experienced for his parents in the process of ego formation. The emotions induced by a patient with preverbal conflicts can also be used in treatment to reduce his sensitivity to similar toxic emotions in highly stressful situations.

CONCLUSION

The analyst who can permit himself to experience the induced feelings, to convert them into toxoid responses, and to communicate these as necessary in the course of resistance analysis, works comfortably with narcissistic patients. As a matter of fact, such an analyst is more comfortable when he works in harmony with the induced emotions than when he tries to suppress them; to keep them out of his interventions would entail the expenditure of considerable energy.

The repeated emotional patterns when felt and experienced in the presence of the analyst are found by both analyst and patient to be the interfering factors that prevent the patient from telling some significant event in his life story or cause him to conceal some painful feeling. The fact that the analyst is able to help the patient recognize that a particular emotional pattern is used to conceal something and that he is able to give the patient the freedom to reveal or not to reveal that information at a particular moment has a therapeutic effect. The patient responds to a setting in which he is helped to feel the motives for his behavior, and particularly if the analyst demonstrates that he wants to know what the patient is concealing, that he understands why the patient is concealing it, and that he is willing to wait for the information until the patient is ready to disclose it voluntarily (Spotnitz, 1967b).

Getting to know the factors that are interfering with the analyst's understanding of the whole life story of his patient as the patient felt and experienced it depends on the willingness of both patient and analyst to experience a range of emotions together, and on their ability to modify their transference resistance and countertransference resistance patterns.

If the practitioner's personality is adapted to this approach, emotional induction operates in his interest as well as in the interest of his patients. A therapy based on the empathetic understanding that develops in the analytic situation is beneficial for the patient and analyst alike. For the recovery of the severely narcissistic person, this type of treatment experience is essential. Ultimately, we shall learn best how to create it.

DREAMS:
The Royal Road
to Preoedipal Conflicts

THE MORE WE LEARN about the human psyche and its conscious and unconscious aspects, the more complex the individual becomes.

Now that the older diagnostic entities are disappearing, we find that a nucleus of obsessive-compulsive traits, character problems, depressive and schizophrenic tendencies, and hereditary and constitutional factors operates in every personality. We are discovering how the intestinal tract, the heart, the skin, and other organs influence the dream. The dream symbolically represents what is going on in the psyche, including knowledge of organ neuroses. If we want to understand the deepest layers of the personality, the most direct route is to study the content of dreams.

Man has speculated on the phenomenon of dreams for centuries and many theories have been advanced to explain why we dream. But until eighty years ago, no one studied dreams scientifically. In July 1895, at the age of 39, Freud had a dream he called "Irma's Injection" to which he later attributed his discovery of the wish-fulfilling function of dreams. Through his work with patients and the analysis of many of his own dreams, Freud uncovered some interesting facts about the structure of dreams. Between 1895 and 1897, he worked on his book, *The Interpretation of Dreams* (1900) and studied his own dreams sporadically. It was this early work that provided us with an answer to why we dream.

Modern analysts ask: What can we agree on that Freud and others have discovered about the dream? There is general agreement that everybody dreams and that dreams occur during sleep. It has been scientifically demonstrated that animals and human beings dream and that dreams are associated with a specific type of brain wave. Not all dreams are remembered when awake. Although it was formerly believed that dreams occurred in either black and white or color, it has recently been hypothesized that dreams may always occur in color: when the emotional content of the dream rises to consciousness, the dreamer realizes he is dreaming in color; when he is avoiding the emotions, he may report that he dreamed in black and white.

Another fact uncovered about dreams is that the dreamer develops an unconscious image or thought into an elaborate production similar to a melodrama or a serious novel. When a person dreams, he experiences the dream as an actual event. If he reports that the dream seemed unreal, part of him was standing off to watch it: in other words, he was placing some distance between himself and the dream.

Not only do we usually experience our dreams as real events, we experience ourselves as not having any free will in the dreams. When a person dreams he is falling through space, for example, he is unable to stop himself from falling. In other words, he is helpless to do anything about the dangerous or unpleasant situations in which he finds himself. Although some dreams represent wish fulfillments, these commonly occur when there is no pressure on the psyche. In dreams we conquer our enemies, and it is safe to do so because we are paralyzed in sleep and cannot engage in the feared impulses that arise from the unconscious. In dreams we can become all-powerful and all-knowing and do all the things we cannot do while awake.

One of Freud's earliest discoveries was that through condensation a number of wishes can be combined in one dream situation. This layering of wishes led Freud to the theory that the deepest wishes—those predating thought—provide the driving force for the creation of dreams and that unraveling the mystery of dreams required a method by which visual imagery could be translated into language. He studied the precognitive ability to condense into one image the different impressions acquired through many experiences. As he began to understand the structure of the dream better, he realized that the dreamer can condense the wishes from various periods of his life into one wish, many situations into one situation, or reverse an emotion into its opposite. Once Freud had discovered and scientifically demonstrated that these mechanisms were used in the construction of dreams, it was possible for future generations to understand why we dream.

Yet despite his insights into the reversals, displacements, and condensations that disguise the dream's latent content, and into how the visual image of the dream is created, Freud found it difficult to complete his book on dream interpretation. His book resisted being written, much as a dreamer resists knowing the disguised message of his dreams.

In the spring of 1897, Freud decided to begin an intensive self-analysis. This decision was partly the result of his determination to complete his book and partly a desire to understand his past. This longing to know the past may have been inspired by his father's sudden death the previous winter. At the time, Freud had few conscious memories of the first three years of his life. In 1898, the year after he began his self-analysis, Freud (1954) wrote the following in a letter to Wilhelm Fliess:

> It seems to me as if the wish-fulfillment theory gives only the psychological and not the biological . . . [explanation of dreams.] . . . Biologically *dream-life seems to me to proceed directly from the residue of the prehistoric stage of life (one to three years) which is the source of the unconscious* and alone contains the aetiology of all the psychoneuroses; the stage which is normally obscured by an amnesia similar to hysteria [p. 246]. . . . . .(*Italics added.*)

> A recent wish leads to a dream only if it can be associated with material from that period, if the recent wish is a derivative of a pre-historic wish, or can get itself adopted by such a wish. I do not know yet to what extent I shall be able to stick to this extreme theory, or let it loose in the dream book [pp. 246-247].

In this letter Freud revealed his conflict about exposing his own preverbal history as well as his theory that a dream cannot occur unless it is a derivative of prehistory. Psychoanalysts now find it easy to define the unconscious as the repressed content of the mind and tend to forget Freud's early definition of the unconscious as the sum of this preverbal period, predating the cognitive functions that use thinking to process the early infantile visual impressions.

In his self-analysis, Freud concentrated on his oedipal conflicts. He unraveled the symbolism of his dreams and, through his associations, studied the connection between his desire for recognition and success, his professional rivalry with colleagues, and his resentment over professional neglect. Although Grinstein (1974) noted the significance of the early preoedipal figures in Freud's dreams, like Freud and others who have written about Freud's dreams, Grinstein was preoccupied with Freud's oedipal wishes. A closer examination of Freud's dreams corroborates his theory that later conflicts which appear in dreams disguise the emotional experiences of the first three years of life that provide the impetus for creating the dream.

When we tackle the disguised meaning of dreams, we encounter the same difficulty that Freud and other psychoanalysts encountered in taking the giant step from repressed verbal memories to never-verbalized early impressions. It is understandable why analysts as well as patients find it so difficult to look at the hidden meaning of dreams. In an earlier letter to Fliess (1898), Freud described his own unconscious as ugly. But, as he pointed out, he was not unique: if everyone could get in touch with the wishes that hide within the depths of the unconscious, we'd find out that people aren't really evil, but that this material does come from a period of life when we're helpless and dependent and are feeling that we cannot cope with the experience we are having.

During his two years of self-analysis, Freud gathered the material that enabled him to complete *The Interpreta-*

tion of Dreams (1900): he resolved his conflict about completing the book and apparently gained much more understanding of his dreams than he revealed in that work. Although he continually hinted at the messages from his own unconscious and brought them to the attention of his colleagues, apparently they did not want to hear these messages.

Like Freud, students of psychoanalysis are confronted with the awesome task of unraveling the meaning of their patient's productions, symptoms, fantasies, and dreams. Freud laid the groundwork for this task in his interpretations of his own dreams. His work of self-analysis invites us to pick up where he left off and perform the analyst's task of corroborating this theory concerning the preoedipal period by unraveling the early origins of his dreams. Freud demonstrated to us how a patient can cooperate by presenting us with the associations and symbols necessary to finish the task of analysis that he had begun alone.

Before looking more closely at Freud's dreams, let us examine his description of the manifest and latent content of dreams. Freud created serious problems for analysts when he said that the dream has a manifest content. Although he developed this artificial construction to introduce his notion of latent content, it tends to confuse us and lead to a false connection between the 'given' and the 'hidden.' The modern analyst looks at the situation differently: What one sees in the dream is the dream; the manifest content is a symbolic expression of the unconscious meaning.

The dream's hidden meaning is not consciously or voluntarily disguised. It is beyond the patient's powers of recall; therefore, it is the manifest dream that provides the road to the individual's unconscious. The latent dream

presented in the associations is what the person remembers and feels at the conscious level. When the
patient reports his associations we learn what he thinks
and feels consciously. But to know what is going on
unconsciously, we must use the manifest content. If the
manifest content can be understood, as it relates to the
content of the session and the associations to the dream,
we can decipher the message from the unconscious. Thus,
when the patient presents a dream, we try to understand
the conscious and the unconscious meaning in both the
manifest and latent content.

Freud's self-analysis revealed the conflicts that developed as a result of emotional experiences during the first
three years of life. He traced the train phobia he suffered
from throughout his life to the traumatic separation from
his homeland at the age of three and to earlier losses
connected with it, and he left us many clues indicating
that he had flirted with breakthroughs to other traumas of
his infancy.

It is interesting to speculate whether Freud's death by
cancer of the jaw could have been averted if he had fully
worked through his depression and its connection with
his early history. For example, we know from his associations that his brother Julius, born when Freud was a year
old, died a year later. We also know that shortly after
Julius' death, Freud fell from his chair, splitting open his
jaw, and that this injury led to major surgery.

FREUD'S DREAMS

The Rome Series. Freud's search for his historical roots
began in the spring of 1897 with the dreams known as the

"Rome Series." A few months earlier his father had died. The Rome dreams demonstrate how current longings for a lost relationship may revive the past and lead to dreaming. In the preface to *Interpretation of Dreams* (1900), Freud connected his regression following his father's death to the early years of his life. During a discussion of the Rome dreams, he mentions his interest in Rome as an example of the inklings of early childhood memories.

In his associations, Freud produced vivid memories of his Catholic nanny who had conversed with him in Czech, a language that as an adult he did not remember. She took him to church every Sunday and he became an avid two-year-old Catholic preaching hell and damnation to the family similar to the way his nurse preached strict discipline to him. As these memories returned, he realized how much he had loved her despite her critical attitude.

In October, 1897, he wrote to Fliess (1954): "The prime originator [of my troubles] was a woman–ugly, elderly, but clever, who told me a great deal about God Almighty and Hell, and who gave me a high opinion of my own capacities." [p.261]

This woman served as Freud's nurse from his birth until he was two and a half years old. We know from Freud's correspondence with Fliess that she was then sent to prison for stealing his kreuzers and zehners, and that his half-brother was responsible for her arrest.

> In the first Rome dream: I was looking out of a railway carriage window at the Tiber, the Ponte Sant' Angelo. The train began to move off and it occurred to me that I had not so much as set foot in the city. [p. 194].

Current wishes for closeness with his friend Fliess and his pending reunion with him in Prague, which again aroused his train phobia, found a basis in earlier longings and provided the foundation for the plot of his dream. The manifest dream content—longings for Rome—symbolized his longings for mothering. Freud's associations led to memories of his nanny and his involvement with her and the church at a time when his mother was preoccupied with the birth of his brother. Reversing the dream thought "set foot in the city" to "set foot out" symbolizes the recognition that he was not his nanny's child and the latent thought, "I should never have been born." The emotional tone of the dream is one of longing and sadness. But Velikovsky (1949), in his paper on Freud's dreams, interpreted the Rome series as revealing Freud's self-hatred based on his Jewishness and his desire to give up his Jewish identification and return to the mother church. Although Velikovsky missed the connection between Catholicism and Freud's nanny, he was a modern analyst in that he recognized the anger that Freud turned against the self when his longings were aroused.

The second dream in the Rome Series continues a theme of unattainability.

> Another time someone led me to the top of a hill and showed me Rome half-shrouded in mist; it was so far away that I was surprised at my view of it being so clear. There was more in the content of this dream than I feel prepared to detail; but the theme of the promised land, seen from afar, was obvious in it [p. 194].

Freud's associations to his Semitic background can be viewed as disguised expression of earlier longings—the longing for the nanny who took him to church and preached to him until he was two and a half years old, and behind this, the longing for his mother. He expressed surprise in his dream that these longings could still be so intense. The visual imagery of Rome from the top of the hill reminds us of the babe's fascination at the breast.

In the third Rome dream, Freud at last gets to Rome:

> There was a narrow stream of dark water; on one side of it were black cliffs and on the other meadows with big white flowers. I noticed a Herr Zucker (whom I know slightly) and determined to ask him the way to the city [p. 194].

Freud's relationships with his male colleagues and the possible connection between those relationships and his early history are revealed in Herr Zucker, a near stranger whom Freud asked to help him find his way to the city. By means of reversal, we can associate stranger with an important person. Freud's associations lead him to thoughts of Charcot and blissful feelings connected with Paris, the city which, despite the hardships, he remembered with longing because Charcot "made up for everything else." At the time of his third Rome dream, Freud planned to meet his friend Fliess in Prague. The name Zucker (sugar) was the connecting link to this trip since he and Fliess planned to discuss the relation between sugar and diabetes.

When we discuss one of Freud's earlier dreams, "Irma's Injection," we shall see that, as Grinstein pointed out (1974), his interest in diabetes as a constitutional disorder is connected with his reference to trymethylamine—a compound that Fliess believed was a sexual by-product excreted in the urine. We will also note Freud's overdetermination of his journey to Prague in relation to his train phobia and the underlying memory of leaving his homeland. By expressing his earlier longings for Austria and by his associations to a later wish for a relationship with Fliess, he reveals the repetitive nature of his searching question: "What must I do to get close to you?"

The fourth dream finds Freud in Rome once more:

> I saw a street-corner before me and was surprised to find so
> many posters in German stuck up there [p. 195].

But in a letter to Fliess (1897), Freud (1954) made several modifications: "I dreamed I was in Rome, walking about the streets and feeling surprised at the large number of German street and shop names." Two new dream thoughts emerged from his study of the associations to this dream. He was struck by the fact that the emotions he experienced for friends and the emotions contained in the Rome dreams could be traced back not only to his nurse but to his German mother. The symbolism of the visual images in this dream (posters stuck up there) is reminiscent of the infant's surprise when he views his mother's body. An investigation of Freud's hobbies and career reveals that the visual memory of the breast is expressed in his longings and search for knowledge and in his love of antiquity. But because his wish to be with his friend Fliess and his longing for their meeting were closer to the surface, they dominated his associations.

Freud's associations to these dreams circumvented the early wishes and instead concentrated in detail on concerns related to his professional life and conflicts based on sibling rivalry. Grinstein (1974), too, interprets these dreams on the oedipal level as a fear of a relationship with nanny (and mother): i.e., as a gratification of oedipal wishes. But we find no indication of a triangle in the material—merely the longing for a mother whose affection is beyond his grasp.

If we view these dreams and Freud's associations to them in their entirety, we see that the longings are presented in symbolic form in the manifest content while the hostile impulses are relegated to the safer sphere of sibling rivalries and appear in the associations. In the Rome Series the depressive element is split—longings in pure form are contained in the manifest content while the narcissistic defense of self-attack dominates the associations. The Freudian view that a dream's manifest content is the disguise and that the associations reveal the unconscious led traditionalists to investigate associations to explain the meaning of the dream. More recently, however, it has become clear that the associations may present additional defenses and disguises, and particularly what is known in the preconscious and conscious mind. The patient tells us the thoughts and impressions he wants known. But to uncover the dream's hidden meaning we must understand the symbolism of the dream itself.

My Son the Myops. A dream recorded in December 1897, carried forth the theme of Freud's early wishes:

A man I knew on the staff of the University said to me: "My son the myops." [Then followed a dialogue made up of short remarks and rejoinders. In the third portion of the dream, the main dream:] On account of certain events which had occurred in the city of Rome, it had become necessary to remove the children to safety, and this was done. The scene was then in front of the gateway, double doors in the ancient style (the "Porta Romana" at Sienna, as I was aware during the dream itself). I was sitting on the edge of a fountain and was greatly depressed and almost in tears. A female figure—an attendant or nun—brought two boys out and handed them over to their father who was not myself. The elder of the two was clearly my eldest son; I did not see the other one's face. The woman who brought out the boy asked him to kiss her goodbye. She was noticeable for having a red nose. The boy refused to kiss her, but, holding out his hand in farewell, said "Auf Geseres" to her and then "Auf Ungeseres" to the two of us (or to one of us). I had a notion that this last phrase denoted a preference [p. 441].

Freud's associations to this dream and Grinstein's discussion of it emphasize Freud's concerns about raising his own children, his feelings about anti-Semitism, his relationship with his father, and his friendship with Fliess. Underlying these concerns, however, we find losses and resentments that occurred during early childhood: his brother Julius' death when Freud was two; his separation from his nurse at age two and a half, the loss at age three of his cousin John, his homeland and all that was familiar; and his mother's pregnancy with his sister Ann during this period. Being replaced at the breast by new-born siblings is a theme in this dream. The female figure, an attendant or nun, has a noticably red nose. A nun with a nipple clearly states the central issue of the dream. That and the Roman door establish a repetitive concern with mothering. The historical sadness of the Jews, symbolized by the fountain (of despair), establishes an emotional tone that is also relatively easy to decipher. The nun is wished a fountain of despair. By this time, Freud had developed a transference to posterity, and he cooperated with us by presenting the manifest content and associations that enable us to understand his early experience.

Up the Stairs. A dream titled "Up the Stairs," which

occurred in May 1897, revealed Freud's conflict about his own birth and the births of his siblings. In a creative reconstruction, he moved away from his usual self-attack to the wish to replace his siblings in utero:

> I was very incompletely dressed and was going upstairs from a flat on the ground floor to a higher storey. I was going up three steps at a time and was delighted [*at my agility*]. Suddenly I saw a maid-servant coming down the stairs—coming towards me, that is. I felt ashamed and tried to hurry, and at this point the feeling of being inhibited set in: I was glued to the steps and unable to budge from the spot [p. 238].

If we substitute "up the stairs" for "down the birth canal," we can see that Freud is taking the stairs "like a man" three stairs at a time—the three stages of birth. As Freud pointed out, the unconscious dream thought is the one based on an emotion. From the day's residue Freud reported that the maid caught him expectorating on the stairs in the home of an old woman whom he visits regularly to administer injections. Dirtying the stairs with his boots, a recent experience, may reflect a present problem—sexual difficulties with his wife—and the past. Placing the dream in a current setting permits "injection" and "maid-servant" to be introduced as a condensation with the past. The maid's appearance in the dream is possible because of Freud's early emotional conflict about his Czech nanny. In analyzing this dream he remembered her harsh treatment and insistence on cleanliness. Like most dreams, this dream relies heavily on displacements, opposites and the use of reversal: e.g., "up the stairs" symbolizes "down the stairs" or "down the birth canal"; the old nursemaid is a substitute for his mother.

In connection with this dream Freud remembers a screen memory in which:

> I saw myself standing in front of a cupboard, demanding something and screaming, while my half-brother, my senior by twenty years, held it open. Then suddenly my mother, looking beautiful and slim walked into the room as if she had come in from the street. These were the words in which I described the scene of which I had a plastic picture, but I did not know what more to make out of it. In analyzing this memory, [my] first associations led to the fact that [I] had missed mother and suspected that she was shut up in the cupboard. I asked my brother to open the cupboard and when he did I began to scream. Then my mother appeared and this allayed my anxiety or longing. But how did I get the idea of looking for my mother in the cupboard * (Freud, pp. 261–266).

The screen memory and Freud's associations shift from birth fantasy to sibling rivalry: "I don't remember what I was demanding." His half-brother's appearance in the screen memory symbolizes his terror of being deprived of his mother as he was of his nurse when his older brother had her imprisoned for stealing. The family's explanation for his nanny's disappearance was that she had been "boxed up," a colloquialism for "sent to prison." Because children take such remarks literally, Freud felt that when his mother disappeared from view, she too was being "boxed up" by his half-brother. One of the passive wishes Freud expressed in the screen memory was that his brother would box him up—Freud's guilt feelings can be viewed in connection with a wish to be boxed up and his screams

* Freud's letter 71 to Fliess, October 1897 discusses this screen memory.

and the terror associated with being in a box. Freud suggested that his brother might have had something to do with not only "boxing up" the nurse but with introducing his newborn sister into his mother's insides. Grinstein (1974) traced the overdetermined quality of his mother's slimness to the birth of his sister Anna, whom Freud undoubtedly had not welcomed. His mother's slimness relieved Freud of the fear of yet another sibling —i.e. there were no more children hidden inside the cabinet. From Freud's preconscious, as revealed in his associations, we begin to understand the resentment of siblings underlying his professional difficulties.

Again the manifest content reveals an early conflict while the associations, including the screen memory, lead us to later conflicts. In a letter to Fliess, Freud reported that a woman came up behind him. When the dream opens, Freud is delighted with his agility, taking three steps at a time (or accomplishing the three stages of labor at once). But his elation ends abruptly when the maid accuses him of expectorating on the stairs. The woman behind is a shadowy figure–mother–the woman awaiting him is critical–maid. Instead of Freud in the act of coitus, we find him caught between two figures in the act. Once again, someone was "boxed up" in his mother. The birth of his sister Anna and the disappearance of his nanny are mysteriously intertwined. A child might conceptualize the act of sexual intercourse as incorporation through "boxing up." Being "glued" to the spot seems to be a way of not being made to disappear. Perhaps it is safer not to be born; if he were in the box now, no new babies would be born. Oedipal wishes are abandoned in favor of earlier wishes. Never being born expresses the wish to be back in the womb away from the critical maid who awaits him outside.

The symbolism of three steps at a time may be related to his explanation of past, present, and future in one image—his birth, fate, and the writing of his book. Freud's delight in his agility turned to shame when confronted with the maid. His associations lead him back to present difficulties. They are a reminder of feelings about the sexual demands of his wife. "This dream confirmed [my] dream theory," he wrote to Fliess.

Irma's Injection. Earlier, in July 1895, in a dream called "Irma's Injection," Freud expressed the feeling that he should never have been born. This dream occurred following a visit from his friend Otto who, after talking with Freud's patient Irma, reported that she was "better but not well." Freud experienced the criticism in Otto's communication. This criticism is reminiscent of the evil old woman who was so critical of him. That evening he went over his notes on Irma's case to determine why she was not more improved. Subsequently, his unconscious delivered a message about what was blocking his progress. Freud recorded the dream as follows:

> A large hall—numerous guests, whom we were receiving. Among them was Irma. I at once took her on one side, as though to answer her letter and to reproach her for not having accepted my "solution" yet. I said to her: "If you still get pains, it's really only your fault." She replied: "If you only knew what pains I've got now in my throat and stomach and abdomen—it's choking me"—I was alarmed and looked at her. She looked pale and puffy. I thought to myself that after all I must be missing some organic trouble. I took her to the window and looked down her throat, and she showed signs of recalcitrance, like some women with artificial dentures. I thought to myself that

there was really no need for her to do that—she then opened her mouth properly and on the right I found a big white patch; at another place I saw extensive whitish grey scabs upon some remarkable curly structures which were evidently modelled on the turbinal bones of the nose—I at once called in Dr. M., and he repeated the examination and confirmed it . . . . Dr. M looked quite different from usual; he was very pale, he walked with a limp and his chin was cleanshaven . . . My friend Otto was now standing beside her as well, and my friend Leopold was percussing her through her bodice and saying: "She has a dull area low down on the left." He also indicated that a portion of the skin on the left shoulder was infiltrated. (I noticed this, just as he did, in spite of her dress.) . . . M. said: "There's no doubt it's an infection, but no matter; dysentery will supervene and the toxin will be eliminated." . . . We were directly aware, too, of the origin of her infection. Not long before, when she was feeling unwell, my friend Otto had given her an injection of a preparation of propyl, propyls . . . propionic acid . . . trimethylamin (and I saw before me a formula for this printed in heavy type) . . . . Injections of that sort ought not be be made so thoughtlessly . . . . And probably the syringe had not been clean [p. 107].

Irma's illness involves the digestive tract and she is choking. Close examination reveals an organic condition—whitish grey scabs in her mouth. Dr. M. agrees with Freud's diagnosis and states that the infection will pass. There was general agreement that the injection which Otto administered (the interpretation of the night before) caused the illness. When discussing the Rome dreams in which Freud meets the stranger, we mentioned that Fliess had discovered the connection between the drug referred to in the dream and sexual by-products in the urine. The injection of a sexual by-product is responsible for Irma's illness. If we interpret these symbols in oedipal terms we find that Freud denies responsibility for his mother's impregnations and that he and his brother (Dr. M.) agree that their father (Otto) gave her "the damaging injection." Freud further complicates his dream by introducing Leopold: Otto's brother and a substitute for Otto. Leopold is more trustworthy. This reminds us of Freud's confusion about his elderly father and his half brother, who was his mother's age and whom Freud considered to be the possible father of his siblings. Dr. M., another dream character, walked with a limp, as did Freud's brother. The emotional tone of this dream is one of guilt, but can we trace the conflict expressed in this dream to an earlier wish? Something that Irma took orally caused the scab-like growths.

Freud (1900) provides us with four clues that enable us to trace this dream to its earliest memories and to the motives which led to it. The first one appears in the following statement:

> My supposition is that a conscious wish can only become a dream instigator if it succeeds in awakening an unconscious wish with the same tenor and in obtaining reinforcement from it .... But these wishes, held under repression, are themselves of infantile origin ... a wish which is represented in a dream must be an infantile one. In the case of adults it originates from the unconsciousness; in the case of children, where there is as yet no division or censorship between the preconscious and the unconscious, or where that division is only gradually being set up, it is

an unfulfilled, unrepressed wish from waking life [pp. 553-554].

Unconscious wishes, always waiting to find expression, ally themselves with an impulse from the conscious waking life and transfer their intensity onto the latter.

Freud's second clue appears as follows: "The most vivid elements of a dream are also those with the most numerous determinants. The greatest intensity is shown by those elements of a dream on whose formation the greatest amount of condensation has been expended" [p. 330].

Freud's (1900) third clue is related to the fact that dreams invariably have more than one meaning. In a footnote added in 1914, he pointed out that "anyone who forgets about the superimposed layering of wishes in dreams will be overlooking one of the most interesting problems in dream interpretation and will easily go astray from understanding the nature of dreams."

And finally, Freud noted that in his experience he had found, without exception, that:

> Every dream deals with the dreamer himself. Dreams are completely egoistic. Whenever my own ego does not appear in the content of the dream, but only some extraneous person, I may safely assume that my own ego lies concealed, by identification, behind this other person, I can assert my ego into the context. On other occasions, when my ego *does* appear in the dream, the situation in which it occurs may teach me that some other person lies concealed, by identification, behind my ego. In that case the dream should warn me to transfer onto myself, when I am interpreting a dream, the concealed common element attached to this other person. But there are also dreams in

which my ego appears along with other people who, when the identification is resolved, are revealed once again as my ego. These identifications should then make it possible for me to bring into contact with my ego certain ideas whose acceptance has been forbidden by the censorship. Thus my ego may be represented in a dream several times over, now directly and now through identification with extraneous persons. By means of a number of such identifications, it becomes possible to condense an extraordinary amount of thought material. . . . When I am in doubt behind which of the figures appearing in the dream my ego is to be looked for, I observe the following rule: The person who in the dream feels an emotion which I myself experience in my sleep is the one who conceals my ego [p. 323].

In his associations, Freud traced the many men and women disguised behind the figures in his dreams to favorite patients and to relatives and colleagues. In a description of one patient and his wish to exchange Irma for her, he tells us everything but the most important fact: whom does Irma symbolize? When Irma is viewed as the disappointing woman (mother), she has been given the wrong injection; thus, Otto is at fault for the way she is. But when Freud asks: "Did I give her the wrong medicine?", i.e., "Was I responsible for her illness?" and when Irma is viewed as his brother Julius, who died when Freud was less than two years old, the same questions can be raised, i.e., "Was I responsible for his illness?"

That night Otto had given Freud a bottle of liqueur which, when opened, smelled like amyl. In the dream the amyl becomes "a propyl," a three carbon chain. We know that the night before this dream, Freud went to bed with the strong feeling that Otto had criticized his treatment methods with regard to Irma, and this aroused Freud's feelings of guilt, perhaps about Julius' death, nanny's imprisonment, etc. In the dream Irma says: "If you only knew how really sick I am."

When we substitute Freud for Irma, we see an inverse oedipal wish. Father gives Freud an injection. Freud defended himself against deeper explorations by avoiding the possible homosexual implications of this dream much as the depressed patient avoids hopelessness by concentrating on his fear of suicide. But when we view Otto as the symbol for Freud's mother, the concentration of oral wishes becomes more meaningful. Otto is substituted, in the manifest content, for mother, who gives Freud the poisoned liqueur and who originally rejected Freud. The chemicals appear in the dream underlined and in capital letters: If we recall Freud's statement that the most vivid elements of a dream are those with the most determinants, then we can see in this dream how the heterosexual, homosexual, and preoedipal elements are condensed: the desire to be boxed up (back in the uterus); fear of being poisoned (criticism and mother's milk); the wish and fear of an injection (a homosexual injection and a feeding).

How can a dream with so many characters be interpreted as a mother-child dream dating back to the time of birth? Freud's clue that the characters in the story line of a dream may be facets of the dreamer's character provide an explanation. Freud felt defective on retiring because of his treatment of his patient. In the dream Irma feels extremely ill. Although the white patches in her mouth are not connected in Freud's associations with thrush, a disease of infancy, this infection is caused by a vaginal infection in the mother and is transferred to the infant during birth and nursing. We must ask: Who is this infant Freud was so concerned about, this infant who was born with an infection? The deepest feelings that Otto's verbal attack aroused in Freud appeared to be: "I am to blame and I am defective" (i.e., anger turned against the self). In the dream Freud set forth the defensive position: Did I give Irma the wrong medicine? Later, however, he projected the blame on Otto who gave her a poisonous injection (the foul-smelling gift). In Freud's repeated self-attack—"I shouldn't trust anyone, I am defective, I should never have been born"—we return to "if Otto (nurse-maid-mother) accuses me, I wish to die." This impulse is condensed with the later wish to take the place of (or annihilate) the unborn siblings of his mother's womb.

The Open Air Closet. The following dream, which Freud called "The Open Air Closet," took place in the summer of 1898:

> A hill on which there was something like an open-air closet: a very long seat with a large hole at the end of it. Its back edges was thickly covered with small heaps of faeces of all sizes and degrees of freshness. There were bushes behind the seat. I micturated on the seat; a long stream of urine washed everything clean; the lumps of faeces came away easily and fell into the opening. It was as though at the end there was still some left [p. 469].

In his associations, Freud connected the dream to the hills and bushes of Ancy, where his children were then vacationing. His preconscious was occupied with thoughts of being a good parent. The dream seemed to remind Freud of Italy, where the water closets in the small towns fit this description. The seat was an exact copy of a piece of furniture a grateful patient had given to him, therefore connecting the toilet seat and feces—a gift as well as excrement. Washing everything clean with urine reminded him of Gulliver, who extinguished the great fire in Lilliput with urine, and of Gargantua, who sat astride Notre Dame and turned his stream of urine upon Paris. In Garnier's painting of Notre Dame, another of Freud's associations, the cathedral is placed on a hill in the center of the painting, rising above small houses and buildings in the foreground.

Despite Freud's conscious nostalgia and concern about his children's future, the symbolism in the dream's manifest and latent content tells a story of aggressive wishes. The entire scene in Garnier's painting is dominated by the giant figure of Gargantua. A large stream of urine descends to the left, down the Seine, carrying with it considerable debris. In the dream, Freud saw a hill on which there was an open air closet, which may be compared to the Notre Dame of the painting. In the dream there is a long seat with a large hole in the end of it; in the painting, Gargantua urinates between the two towers of Notre Dame. In the dream, Freud urinates on the seat, washing everything clean: i.e. Freud identified with Gargantua. In another connection, Freud spoke of his desire to be a great man like Gargantua. In the symbol of urinating on the mother, we see what the great man has in mind: Freud's preconscious associations reveal the aggressive intent of extinguishing the sexual fires in his mother and of annihilation of excrement, accompanied by a description of himself as human filth.

In Freud's dream, the omnipotent fantasies of early childhood are fulfilled on a grand scale—urinating on all Paris and superman astride his mother. His associations led him to the tiny queen in *Gulliver's Travels* who did not appreciate Gulliver's action of putting out the fire with his urine, but instead punished him with a tongue lashing. The dream presents the conflict between impulses of power, exaggerated self-assertion, and feelings of helplessness and worthlessness. Freud's associations to the dream reveal his underlying depression: a worthless man wallowing in human filth. The black hole from which he emerged was a condensation of memories of Italy, antiquity, and mother. His solution was to wash the feces back in. His hopelessness is revealed in the last sentence of the dream: "there was still some left." This two-character dream reveals little concern about castration but tremendous rage at his mother, who looms large and sensual and continues to pour forth more filth to replace Freud.

Non Vixit. In his dream "Non Vixit" and in the associations related to it, Freud again expressed the wish to be rid of troublesome rivals:

> I had gone to Brücke's laboratory at night, and in response to a gentle knock on the door, I opened it to *(the late)* Professor Fleischl, who came in with a number of strangers and, after exchanging a few words, sat down at his table. This was followed by a second dream. My friend Fl. [Fliess] had come to Vienna unobtrusively in July. I met him in the street in conversation with my *(deceased)* friend P., and went with them to some place where they sat opposite each other as though they were at a small table. I sat in front at its narrow end. Fl. spoke about his sister and said that in three-quarters of an hour she was dead, and added some such words as "that was the threshold." As P. failed to understand him Fl. turned to me and asked me how

much I had told P. about his affairs. Whereupon, overcome by strange emotions, I tried to explain to Fl. that P.
(could not understand anything at all, of course, because
he) was not alive. But what I actually said—and I myself
noticed the mistake— was, "NON VIXIT." I then gave P.
a piercing look. Under my gaze he turned pale; his form
grew indistinct and his eyes a sickly blue—and finally he
melted away. I was highly delighted at this and I now
realized that Ernst Fleischl, too, had been no more than an
apparition, a "revenant," and it seemed to me quite possible that people of that kind only existed as long as one
liked and could be got rid of if someone else wished it [p.
421].

On the surface this dream deals with the unveiling of
a memorial to Fleischl; but being seated at the table
reveals Freud's continuing interest in the breast. By inad-
vertently substituting "non vixit" (he never existed) for
"non vivit" (he is not alive), Freud vanquished in an
instant those who annoyed him. (Freud may have envied
the "magic powers" his half-brother displayed by "van-
quishing" the nanny in an instant.)

The Three Fates. One of the concluding dreams in
Freud's personal analysis, "The Three Fates," occurred
after his summer vacation in 1898. Actually, this dream
ends the series that uncovered the early infantile material
and reveals Freud's annoyance about his mother's seductiveness when what he desired was affection.

I went into a kitchen in search of some pudding. Three
women were standing in it; one of them was a hostess of
the inn and was twisting something about in her hand as
though she were making Knödel [dumplings]. She an-

swered that I must wait till she was ready. (*These were not definite spoken words.*) I felt impatient and I went off with a sense of injury. I put on an overcoat. But the first I tried on was too long for me. I took it off, rather surprised to find it was trimmed with fur. A second one that I put on had a long strip with a Turkish design let into it. A stranger with a long face and a short pointed beard came up and tried to prevent my putting it on, saying it was his. I showed him then that it was embroidered all over with a Turkish pattern. He asked: "What have the Turkish (designs, stripes . . .) to do with you?" But then we became quite friendly with each other [p. 204].

*

My dream of the three fates was clearly a hunger dream. But it succeeded in shifting the craving for nourishment back to a child's longing for his mother's breast, and it made use of an innocent desire as a screen for a more serious one which could not be so openly displayed.

Here Freud stressed his craving for nourishment as a disguise for oedipal longings. His associations led him to the death of Fleischl, a colleague, and his brother, and we may assume that behind this lies the association to his wish that Julius either had not been born or would die. The woman twisting something in her hands reminded Freud of the inevitability of death and of his mother's instruction that he must wait for food. Frustration is followed by the putting on of identities. Although the oedipal meaning may be gleaned from this, as Grinstein suggests, it is more likely since food is the object of his desire, that he took the identity of a sibling (a little Turk) and offered himself to his mother sexually to seduce her into breast feeding him. He has a special French tickler, the overcoat with Turkish design, with which to excite and seduce her.

The immediate resentment that may have stimulated this dream was related to his wife's demand that he "wait for her" sexually. As in his associations to the two previous dreams, Freud revealed in his associations to this one that as he proceeded with his self-analysis, his wishes were less disguised in both the manifest and the latent content. Death in unity with mother dominates the dream's associations. In the "open air closet" anger at his mother's seductiveness was expressed in his association to Gulliver who put out the city's fires. His anger at his mother's fertility is present also in associations to these dreams.

Freud's associations brought to mind the three fates who spin the destiny of man. The hostess at the inn is the mother who gives life. Love and hunger meet at a woman's breast. The woman who bears him, the woman who is his mate, and the woman who destroys him are the three inevitable relationships in a man's life. The association to the woman rubbing her hands together as though making dumplings led Freud to recall one of his mother's first lessons. When he was six, she told him that man is made of earth and returns to earth.

> When I expressed doubts at this, my mother rubbed her palms together as she did in the making of the dumplings, except that there was no dough between them and she showed me the blackish scales of *epidermis* produced by the friction, as a proof that we were made of earth. . . . *I acquiesced in the belief that we were made of earth.*

Freud connected this memory with submission to

the inevitable and then recalled the university where he had spent his happiest hours at the "breast of wisdom-"—associations to Brucher and to Fleischl (meaning meat, which, like knödel, is something to eat). Associations to Fleischl and knödel may be said to connect the theme of orality as oral sadistic impulses directed against his mother.

CONCLUSION

Freud taught us that dreams represent a return to the beginnings of our own development and reveal our most hidden self as well as the most infantile sources of our existence and each person's unique history.

He stated (1900):

> We have not only found that the material of the forgotten experiences of childhood is accessible to dreams, but we have also seen that the mental life of children with all its characteristics, its egoism, its incestuous choice of love objects, and so on, still persists in dreams—that is, in the unconscious, and that dreams carry us back every night to this infantile level. The fact is thus confirmed that what is unconscious in mental life is also what is infantile. The strange impression of there being so much evil in people begins to diminish. This frightful evil is simply the initial, primitive, infantile part of mental life, which we can find in actual operation in children [p. 218].

The day's residues connect a wish in the person's current life with a wish from his prehistory. Dreams, fantasies, and symptoms tell us what a patient knows but cannot say. By silent analysis of these productions, we will discover what corrective experience is required to reverse the emotional repetition. It is only by understanding what the patient originally lacked in his environment that we will know how to keep him growing in the present. But we must remember that a patient is not cured by understanding his own emotional state. Much more is required. The analyst must be willing to know the patient, to know what was lacking in his early environment, and to know what emotional response today will remove the patient's resistance to mature functioning.

Through some miraculous means not yet clearly understood, when we understand the patient, he begins to understand himself. It is usually the analyst who holds up the patient's progress because he is unable to conquer his own countertransference and understand the patient. But when the analyst genuinely understands him, the patient has little difficulty following the analyst's lead.

By 1899 Freud was free to remember, in disguised form, the most emotionally significant events of the first three years of his life, but unfortunately the disguise was never lifted. He was destined to repeat those early events — lost objects for whom he felt longing, hate, and desire for revenge; eventual loss of friends and homeland; increased self-blame; and depression and somatic self-attack which culminated in his death from cancer of the jaw, as predicted in "Irma's Injection." Some of his symptoms were reversed, however. By the summer of 1899 he had traced his symptom of bedwetting to its early source and recognized the relationship between his train phobia and early losses. And finally, he was able to trace his mania, somatizing, and depression to feelings of frustration about the neglect of his oral needs and, later, to feelings concerning his mother's seductiveness.

At first, Freud attempted to approach dreams on the symbolic level, but later he favored a theory of latent and manifest contents in which he interpreted the manifest as the disguise. Modern analysts emphasize the symbolism of the dream as the clue to its meaning and recognize that associations continue the disguise of early memories, revealing only what the dreamer wants to know.

The manifest content of Freud's dreams contained all the information necessary to understand his unconscious. His earliest memories are there: longing for mothering, loss of love, bitterness, feelings of worthlessness that were developed to protect him from his awareness of disappointment in love, and infantile fantasies of revenge and power. His associations help us to unravel the symbolism and corroborate the message of the manifest content by showing us how he repeated these conflicts later in life in the form of a search for wisdom and in disappointment with colleagues.

PART II
Technical
Considerations

By instruction and demonstration through books, courses, and seminars, only the *technicalities* of the psychoanalytic profession can be learned.

The most important aspects of *technique* must be experienced .. not until he knows just how far these technicalities go, and knows them utterly, ... only when he thoroughly understands the peculiarities of his tools and has practiced their use for a long time, does he come to the point where he need no longer concern himself with them.

Theodor Reik
1949, p. 48.

THE TREATMENT PARTNERSHIP

U NDERGOING PSYCHOANALYSIS is an enormous
task. The psychoanalytic process requires a period of time in which the analysand may present
a certain type of material for inspection by the psychoanalyst. The flow of the material is determined by the
unconscious and the defense structure of the analysand.
The analysand on the couch is in a position that affords
cooperative relaxation. The tendency to relax and be
comfortable, which is stimulated by the comparatively
uniform surroundings in which the patient finds himself
during the analytic hours, is disturbed by whatever past
experiences have caused a state of excitement within him.
This disturbing tendency, an attempt at the discharge of
previously stored up emotional tension, is ordinarily held
in check by the demands of reality. In the analysis the
patient is invited to put everything into words and to
suspend other voluntary activity. With this restriction,
the patient reveals his characterological patterns as the
analysis unfolds.

Aberrations of character, behavior disorders, neurotic
and psychotic difficulties and many other types of emo-

tional disturbances that plague so many people have long since ceased to be regarded, as they were for many centuries, as caused by evil spirits or other mysterious forces. A long time ago, we stopped stoning the emotionally disturbed to death, burning them at the stake, or keeping them shackled in dark dungeons. We know that their conditions are essentially illnesses and that, like most other illnesses, they respond to proper treatment. We are also aware that these people cannot be expected to cure themselves. The cure of emotional disturbances will require the united efforts of psychoanalysts and psychiatrists, psychologists and psychiatric social workers, and all other mental health counselors.

Emotional health, like emotional illness, can be contagious. Parents rarely mistreat their children consciously or deliberately; but only those who are themselves emotionally healthy can give their children the proper psychological nourishment—the love and parental care that catalyze sound emotional growth.

Viewed in perspective, our scientific understanding of emotional growth, and our development of the techniques needed for influencing human behavior through psychoanalytic methods of treatment, are very new acquisitions indeed. It is only within the last seventy years that we have begun to make any constructive effort to cope with mental illness.

Before he can begin to treat emotional disturbance, the analyst is trained to understand motivation and defense. Knowing the character of patients precedes decisions about technical interventions.

A long time ago,* the Greek prophet Tiresias, described the

*Reprinted by permission of the *Psychoanalytic Review.*

fate of three men which has an important significance for psychoanalysts today. His first prediction concerned the future of an infant, the son of a beautiful nymph named Liriope and the river god who first raped her and then cast her aside. The worried mother had come to Tiresias to learn what prospect Destiny held for the unwanted infant in her arms. "Would the child," asked Liriope, "live to a ripe old age?" "He would be so blessed," Tiresias replied, "if he n'er knows himself."

The infant grew into the beautiful youth named Narcissus, who rejected the love of every young man and every young woman he met, and then became so aflame with love of his own reflection in a pool of water that he could not tear himself away from the vision and finally withered away in self-neglect.

The second prediction was made to a father—a Greek king. He was warned that his life and throne were endangered by the son who was about to be born to him. And despite all of the king's efforts to avert this danger, the prophecy of Tiresias was fulfilled: Years later it came to pass that this son unknowingly slew his father, married his mother and had children with her. In the searing words of the Greek dramatist Sophocles, Oedipus became the "heir to his father's bed, shedder of his father's blood, at once brother and father of his children, and son and husband of the woman who bore him."

The wrong kind of sexual love—incest—is as deadly as too much love of oneself, Tiresias was saying.

The third prediction is recorded in one of the oldest novels preserved to Western civilization—Homer's great story, *The Odyssey*. You will recall that Odysseus—or Ulysses, as he is better known—sailed away from his home and family to spend ten years fighting the Trojan War.

Nine more years were to pass before he saw home again. Ulysses roamed far and wide and, even though he was under the protection of the bright-eyed goddess Athena, he suffered many hardships in his efforts to get his men home safely and preserve his own life. Ulysses' long absence from home caused many difficulties for his devoted wife, forced his son to grow up without a father's care, turned his own father into a melancholy recluse, and broke his mother's heart. She died grieving for her son and his "wise and gentle ways."

By this time, Tiresias' own life had come to an end, but death had not robbed him of his power to foretell the future. In the course of his long voyage home, Ulysses stopped off in the Halls of Hades to consult the soul of the blind seer. Tiresias warned him that the trip ahead would be long and hard, with many mishaps; the blind seer's ghost also explained how he should propitiate the gods. And finally, it was predicted that Ulysses would be reunited with his family, and live for many years thereafter. Death would come to him in its "gentlest guise," Ulysses was told, when he was "worn out after an easy old age and surrounded by prosperous people."

Homer celebrates Ulysses as a man of sound judgment, nimble wit, and indomitable courage, a man whom "nothing defeats." Despite his wandering spirit and the suffering he brought to his family, Ulysses made an adjustment to reality which was admirable for his life and time, one which met with the approval of his society. That was why Tiresias predicted for Ulysses three thousand years ago what men and women have always needed and shall go on needing to give a sense of fulfillment to their lives. These needs are, in essence, a happy family, an easy old age and fortunate living circumstances for themselves and others.

Patients will often recall directly, or in the symbols of the dream or fantasy, the unconscious craving of early childhood for the parent of the opposite sex. The infantile sexual impulses, manifested in what has come to be known as the family romance—more ubiquitously the Oedipus complex—are frequently the source of deep disturbance that must be resolved in treatment. Early in the development of psychoanalysis sexual impulses were difficult to accept, but they were understood in relation to maturity and love more readily than were the destructive impulses.

Every analyst has contact at one time or another with a Ulysses in modern dress, the personality whose wanderlust drives him hither and yon, pursuing some dim vision of happiness. The vision itself is usually out of reach, and the members of his own family are never a part of his plans. Such a person has to learn that one does not gain the deeper satisfaction of life by spending all one's time searching for them, but as a byproduct, more often than not unintended, of creative and socially productive activities.

Many a patient recalls Narcissus, excessively absorbed in himself, and seemingly incapable of meaningful emotional attachments to the people and things in his environment. That is why the Narcissus myth has come to be regarded as an object-lesson in the suicidal effect of too much absorption in oneself—what we generally refer to as pathological narcissism.

These predictions have a special significance today for the psychoanalyst, who repeatedly experiences in his practice the emotional currents symbolized by the names of Narcissus, Oedipus and Ulysses.

THE PSYCHOANALYST

Beginning with Freud, psychoanalysis has identified itself with mythology for a very important reason. The myth of the hero in search for meaning is the cornerstone of every psychoanalysis. To take the path of the hero was Freud's special ability, described so movingly in his early works as he struggled through to an understanding of his own oedipal conflicts. Psychoanalysis was built on the model of Freud's search for self-understanding. Treatment was designed as an introspective process in which the sine qua non was re-experiencing one's emotional history and understanding how it repeats itself in the present. As the mythical struggle of the hero is an emotional voyage, so psychoanalysis is an emotional re-experiencing of old truths.

As the analyst begins to work with his patients, he learns to value and accept the unfolding of another's personality. Discussing man's nature with Lionel Trilling, Jones (1948) suggested that rather than do away with the "monster" we should face the unconscious depths of lust, hate, and pettiness within us all. Flugel (1970) described the task of the psychoanalyst as one of helping a patient face his own nature and fate, allowing the patient the freedom to fully express his emotions, "and this is opposed to those attitudes which stress the importance of moral control and urge us to avoid any thoughts which will put this control in jeopardy."

Wilson (1967), warned that "the method of averting one's attention from evil and simply living in the light of the good is splendid as long as it will work . . . but there is no doubt that healthy-mindedness is inadequate as a philosophical doctrine."

Fromm (1947), considering the lot of man wrote:

> He is born at an accidental point in time. His life span limits his participation in human development to this one point in the historical process, and this must conflict with his claim for the realization of his potentialities . . . . If a man faces his fundamental aloneness in a universe indifferent to his fate and recognizes that there is no meaning to life except the one he gives it by the unfolding of his powers . . .

But, even before the analyst addresses himself to the task, he begins his own odyssey. As we examine the heroic efforts of Freud to understand himself, we see that even this hero could not achieve full self-knowledge, as he himself recognized late in his life. We saw his struggles in the early decades of the twentieth century with "the stone wall of narcissism"; we saw his failure with cases such as that of Dora when he was unable to deal with the revenge motive in her personality, and we saw his own eventual defeat by cancer.

Much of our work in the analysis of our patients is concerned with getting in touch with our own unresolved conflicts. Since the analyst brings his own personality to the treatment relationship in his countertransference response to the patient's transference, his inner freedom becomes an issue of prime importance. By undertaking psychoanalytic training, the analyst declares his intention to undertake the heroic odyssey to know himself. Reik (1952) discussing subjective countertransference wrote, "It is vital that the mirror that we hold up to the patient is not itself distorted. It is the wise analyst who is constantly alert to fresh arousal of problems not previously taken up in his own analysis in depth." Hopefully, personal analysis will safeguard the analyst from overlooking the signs of subjective feelings interfering with the transference of the patient.

Training the student of psychoanalysis to work with these feelings is the cornerstone of modern psychoanalysis. Until the modern analyst is thoroughly in touch with his own feelings and the feelings induced in him by the patient and can delay acting on them, he cannot train patients to do the same.

Furthermore, an analyst must have the ability to live in the present. This involves the capacity for emotional closeness, particularly at levels in which the preoedipal strivings of the patient arouse similar strivings on the part of the analyst. The analyst who can tolerate the patient's strong impulses and experience the appropriate feelings creates the maturational environment in which induced negative and positive feelings are conveyed to the patient only at the appropriate time.

One patient described analysis as "like a religion of love." The patient can leave when he wants to, he gets the right emotional food, both positive and negative, and the feeding is appropriately timed.

Analysts have always recognized the necessity for a personal analysis for those who will work with the emotions of others. As Reik (1935) pointed out, "A sorcerer's apprentice can never duplicate the magician's feats. And neither will mechanical observation make an analyst." Reik believed that, "The essential matter of psychoanalysis is lived with not learned."

The analyst who uses himself as a technical instrument is participating in a tension-producing task. He creates a balance between the frustrations of the psychoanalytic situation and the verbal gratification that will bring all the latent transference emotions to full expression.

The student analyst soon learns how much easier it is to stifle the emotion by giving a gratifying communication that relieves the patient in his suffering or to act mechanically with his patient in order to avoid his own depths of feeling. Avoidance is far simpler than working through emotional stress in which the very person of the analyst is the subject of attack. The analyst's ability to tolerate his own and the patient's frustration and negative feelings, the patient's total devotion to an all-powerful object and his own positive and protective feelings aroused during sessions, without trying to "make things better", is the carefully-trained talent about which Reik wrote. These qualities can be learned by the person with sensitivity to the maturational needs of another. It is "the innate gift without which all training is a waste" (Reik, 1948).

Because of his belief that the practice of psychoanalysis requires intuition and talent, Fritz Perls emphasized the selection of candidates with a literary rather than scientific background, concluding that the future analyst and the writer possess the same inclination to character analysis.

Bergler (1958) defined the difference between writer and analyst as follows: "The writer creates the actions of his marionettes from his own unconscious, makes them act correctly without knowing why.... The analyst is provided with these actions which he must interpret correctly in full knowledge of the determining reasons by the patient. The writer must, without knowing it, accomplish what the psychoanalytic psychiatrist achieves consciously: the correct interpretation of human reactions" [p. 95].

Most psychoanalytic educators recommend a four to six-year graduate training program for psychoanalysts, suggesting that from the standpoint of mental training, the study of medicine or any of the exact sciences is not necessarily the best preparation for the candidate. More desirable is a general education that has been as wide and varied as possible, acquainting the candidate with the great variety of capabilities and activities of the human mind, and providing him with some understanding of them.

Because the withdrawn patient absorbs the feelings of others and, in fact, finds it difficult to separate them from his own, the analyst must remain constantly aware of what he himself is feeling and why (Nagelberg *et al.*, 1953). Feeling tones which would not be therapeutic for him to communicate, however unwittingly, must be screened out. Others are developed through a searching self-study and a deeper understanding of all factors that have led to the patient's deviant mental and social functioning. Technical proficiency is of little avail if it does not help the analyst to develop in himself the kind of feelings that will catalyze the release of his emotional energy in language.

THE NARCISSISTIC PATIENT

However circuitously he begins, the narcissistic patient pours out his most intimate thoughts and feelings in the course of treatment. The communication of personal data remains a one-way process, despite the patient's often overwhelming desire for a reciprocal flow of confidences. At times it is difficult for his partner to maintain the attitude which the situation dictates: psychological aloofness regarding himself combined with mild but genuine interest in everything the patient says about himself. This apparent impersonality led one narcissistic youth, when he could permit himself to be critical of his analyst, to accuse him of being a "logical piece of machinery" (Spotnitz *et. al.,* 1956).

Initially the narcissistic patient does not think of his analyst as a man of feeling who labored to develop his capacity as an analyst or as one who experiences doubts about his effectiveness, or has feelings of despair and hopelessness. The analyst appears to Narcissus as a god-like figure who functions either automatically or mechanically, or out of divine wisdom.

Were the analyst actually the mechanically functioning and unfeeling instrument of the patient's fancy, treatment would be far easier to administer. What the patient fails to perceive is that his analyst is an ordinary human being carrying on a type of activity that makes stringent demands on his own personality. For what are incidental and extraneous factors in all other organized forms of remedial activity—the analyst's personality and the behavior he manifests minute after minute, his unexpressed thoughts and feelings as well as his words—are the tools the psychoanalyst uses in his treatment.

As the analyst administers the carefully measured and graduated dosages of emotional communication that a severely withdrawn person requires, this malleable instrument is itself being exposed to certain non-therapeutic tensions and reactions induced by the patient's pathological behavior patterns. These can create serious problems for one who is dealing with a patient as hyper-sensitive to the feelings of others as is a withdrawn child or narcissistic adult. It is much easier for an añalyst to limit his verbal communications and to control his other actions in a treatment session than to prevent his mental attitudes and reactions from being sensed by his patient. Unlike one-way communications, influences flow in both directions during the session, and they too can boomerang.

To keep track of all the emotional forces at work inside the patient, inside himself, and criss-crossing from one to the other, an analyst has to become a spectator at a four-ring circus. He must carefully observe, in ring one, the patterns of actions, impulses and feeling that were inculcated in his companion before they met. The equi-valent patterns established in the analyst as a result of his own early life experiences are delineated in ring two. Therapeutic activity could be planned and conducted more easily if these two rings were all that had to be kept in view. But there are two more rings; analysis is a four-ring circus full of intricate performances to be watched. In ring three, the emotional forces that the analyst's personality and behavior induce in the patient are in action. Conversely, in ring four, those which the latter's personality and behavior induce in the analyst can be seen.

These emotional forces unceasingly battle among themselves for supremacy as they attempt to control the behavior of the two partners in therapy. To prevent them from interfering with therapy, and to synchronize their performances with the goals of treatment, constant sur-veillance of all rings is essential.

The analyst who has had sufficient personal psychoanalysis is assumed to be well aware of his own
customary forms of behavior and mental activity; he is
conscious of his own personal assets and liabilities and has
an objective understanding of the impression they make
upon other individuals. It is harder for him, though, to
detect if and when and how his own behavior and attitudes may alter as he is experiencing the markedly deviant
behavior and attitudes of the withdrawn patient. To
function properly as his own instrument of therapy, he
must be able to recognize and cope with any emotional
currents that may be interfering with this subjective
instrument, and could even pull it off its charted course.

It is recommended that in the opening phase of
treatment of the narcissistic case, the patient be provided
with as non-stimulating and as controlled a setting as
possible. No pressure is exerted. The analyst does not talk
unnecessarily because of his own theoretical understanding of the withdrawn person's tendency to experience the
mere impact of another personality as a constraining force.
Furthermore, the narcissistic patient requires a constant
and tension-free environment, one in which he feels safe
in forming a relationship with another human being. This
means approaching him with great emotional reserve.
Any display of affectionate concern may further disrupt
his functioning, whereas an attitude of restrained interest
on the part of the analyst keeps the patient in a state of
mild comfort, just enough to make him want to struggle
for more.

Until he is fully ready to do so, however, the patient is
allowed to put as much distance between himself and the
therapist as he himself, through his own behavior, indi-

cates is essential to keep him in fair equilibrium. This serves as reassurance to him that his fears of his inability to control his own impulsiveness are understood by his analyst, who is helping him to prevent himself from harming either one of them. Insulated doubly–by his own tendency to withdraw from external stimuli, and by the relative non-existence of these stimuli in the treatment relationship–the patient is then able to use his therapy sessions as a sort of mental training-ground, equipped with all conceivable safety devices. There he can practice releasing his destructive impulses in language until he becomes proficient in discharging them in a controlled and measured way. Once that is possible, the emotional withdrawal which had been maintained at such great psychic cost to himself can be abandoned since feelings that do not lead to dangerous actions do not have to be nullified or modified. Investing emotions in interchanges with understanding partners is then a harmless, and even an enjoyable way of learning how to live in and with society.

Those, in summary, are some clinical hypotheses that the analyst keeps in mind when he begins treatment of a patient. To accept these hypotheses intellectually is not enough; real feelings about the patient, negative as well as positive, have to be developed. Sincerity as well as spontaneity of response is vital, but the kind of response that the narcissistic personality's antipathetic behavior customarily evokes in others hardly leads to the establishment of good rapport, nor does it tempt him to emerge from his own non-feeling state and trust himself to feel and talk about his own thoughts, feelings and impulses. On the contrary, he tries to pull the analyst into the same type of unreal functioning as his own. This is one of the principal dangers that have to be faced in working closely with a pathologically narcissistic personality: the necessity of developing an objective understanding of the patient's deviant behavior so that it might be responded to with the appropriate feelings. The analyst may have to overcome a tendency to feel neither love nor hatred before he can respond appropriately to the patient's expressions of self-hatred and contempt, his asocial and excessively impulsive behavior. It must be stressed that, whether or not it would be therapeutic to show this dislike in a particular situation, unless the therapist is able to experience these feelings, he cannot fully understand what motivates the pattern of behavior or feeling with which he has to contend.

THE ANALYST INTERVENES

PSYCHOANALYSIS HAS been defined variously as a metapsychology, a research method, a body of empirical knowledge, a theory of treatment and a treatment technique.

As a metapsychology, it has developed such notions as the unconscious, instinct theory, and id-ego-superego. As a body of knowledge, it has outlined patterns of human behavior and interaction in the stages of man's development from conception to death. As a method of investigation it has utilized verbal communication and the analytic session as a means through which human interaction may be decoded and understood. As a theory of treatment and treatment technique, it has developed concepts to explain what leads to cure, and techniques, which when applied, do allow one person to assist in the emotional maturation of another.

Freud observed clinically that people in treatment have a compulsion to repeat early-learned ways of responding and that as adults they respond to new situations in these habitual ways. A patient brings into his sessions the characterological patterns with which he has learned to relate to others.

If a sufficient emotional transference is made by the patient to the psychoanalyst, the resulting transference neurosis can be cured by therapeutic work. Freud found that this affective relationship must exist in order to prevent the patient from taking flight when painful matters come to his awareness. Although these emotional reactions relate to the patient's early family relationships, they are experienced for the psychoanalyst himself. This state was viewed as "an intermediary realm between illness and reality,". . . peculiar "in both character and degree over what is rational and justifiable" (Freud, 1912). The idea of an emotional involvement of patient with analyst in which the past is brought into the present provided the groundwork for psychoanalytic technique.

When a transference has "developed into a sufficiently strong attachment," according to Freud (1912), "treatment is in a position to prevent all the more important of the patient's repetitious actions and to make use of his intentions alone as material for the therapeutic work." Freud hastened to add that although we "allow the transference the right to assert itself within certain limits, the handling of the transference is the analyst's main instrument for curbing the patient's compulsion to repeat."

When the analyst attempts to analyze the transference, he finds that patients seem unwilling to give up the satisfaction gained from illness, so that even the transference itself must be regarded as a resistance to cure. By merging psychoanalyst, self, and early objects, current emotional reactions become a substitute for progressive communication, remembering, and working through.

Wilhelm Reich (1949) emphasized the resolution of

the resistance and the analysis of the transference as the most important analytic work. "Don't nip resistances in the bud," he wrote, "but bring them to full development in the transference situation so that full affects which are transferred can be utilized."

We recognize that in the early phase of treatment the patient has come to ease his pain, not to change his character. He is not interested in getting in touch with longings or destructive thoughts or feelings toward the analyst even though he may complain about the kind of treatment he receives from others. He resists by behaving impulsively (id resistances), self-attack (superego resistances), pleasure (or secondary gain resistances), and asserting himself (ego resistances). When these are related to the analysis and the analyst, they become transference resistances. Freud's structural insights into transference and resistance were based on the neurotic psychic structure.

The understanding of the narcissistic transference developed later through work with preoedipal phases in the maturation process.

Spotnitz (1969b), in discussing preoedipal conflicts, described what is repressed as the prefeelings of hatred and its discharge. Although early situations may be remembered, the aggressive impulses are forgotten. The repetition compulsion aroused in narcissism is dominated by the longing to be touched. Murderous, unforgiving rage for the denying early object alternates with cravings for contact and affection. We call it id resistance when the patient acts on these impulses to annihilate, to be held or to be fed by transference figures. Ego resistances are disturbances of the cognitive processes. In narcissism, the following inappropriate affects may be used for defensive purposes: feelings of emptiness, danger, resentment, eerie feelings, and the absence of feeling, as well as blocked thoughts or confused, jumbled thinking. The secondary gain resistance in schizophrenia may be gratification of dependency feelings, and in depression, gratification of the need for punishment. The preoedipal patient employs superego resistances, immersing himself in feelings of incurability, worthlessness and hopelessness.

These defenses are used by the narcissistic patient to oppose growth. When they become a part of the reactions to the analyst and are fully charged with affect they become narcissistic transference resistances. Resolving resistances awaits an understanding of them as they are manifested as transference resistances.

TREATMENT-DESTRUCTIVE RESISTANCE

In some cases, the patient resists the transference by attempting to break the relationship. The fears behind treatment-destructive behavior relate to the fear of forming a new relationship. The transference relationship is one in which old fears and wishes will be aroused along with the maladaptive ways of seeking gratification. We understand the importance of treatment-destructive behavior to the psychic economy when it is recognized as resistance to experiencing a negative transference.

In the beginning, the analyst's concern is with how the patient resists the negative transference and how to prevent the arousal of more negative transference than the patient can tolerate. The early goal is accomplished primarily through silent investigation and communications that modify the intensity of the frustration. During this period the patient silently considers the value of the treatment.

Modern analysts encourage a negative transference in which ego resistances (destruction of the mental functions), and id resistances (threats of leaving or other relationship-destructive action), will be kept to a minimum by limiting the arousal of thoughts and feelings to a quantity that is tolerable. In the treatment-destructive phase a patient's very existence seems threatened by feelings for the analyst or those projected to the analyst. One patient reported, "I feel like I'm letting more and more of you into me. It seems like I'm more afraid of fighting with you now. I'm more afraid of losing you." The patient's comments were appropriate to the transference situation since the more the analyst means to the patient, the more the fear of loss is aroused. A narcissistic patient asked, "How can you be so important to me? I don't even have you, just one hour a week and then only a voice. There is no reality here except inside my head. The important realities are time and space." This type of object-oriented communication will alternate in sessions with narcissistic transference communications and narcissistic transference resistances. Following a discussion of the oedipal realities of time and space, this patient described his transference: "I'm in danger here. I may destroy you, but I feel it as if I'll be destroyed. I don't know which, but you have power. I feel I have not been born yet." (This showed a negative narcissistic transference.)

Reich (1949) observed that a spontaneous transference develops if the analyst avoids giving interpretations too early or too deep. It is possible, in a psychoanalytic method that de-emphasizes interpretation, for the patient to move quite naturally to a transference neurosis. Each resolution of treatment-destructive resistances is made through the maintenance of a neutral environment. Other defenses are actively maintained while the analyst investigates the function they serve. Toward this end, a number of techniques have been developed for reflecting and joining the resistances. As each resistance is explored and joined, more of the original problem is verbalized in the transference. Eventually what led to the narcissistic fixation is verbalized. Early in treatment, communication on these matters is mainly symbolic.

Ferenczi (1950) was one of the first of Freud's followers to recommend alternative techniques to interpretation. He had observed that there were certain types of patients who could not be cured by conventional means. He also discovered that there were periods of stagnation in analysis, during which new techniques were needed to hasten the exploration of unconscious material. In the case of an hysterical woman who used onanistic substitutes, he forbade masturbation. "I was compelled," he wrote, "to give up the passive part that the psychoanalyst is accustomed to play in the treatment, which is confined to the hearing and interpretation of the patient's ideas, and had, by active interference in the patient's psychic activities, to help her over dead points in the work of the analysis" [p. 201].

Ferenczi had noted many devices used by patients to resist cure. He observed how difficult it was for the patient to follow the first rule of free flow of ideas until close to the end of the analysis, and that patients could not understand that free association did not demand complete thinking out of ideas, but complete utterance of what was actually thought.

Ferenczi explained how active technique works in

bringing unconscious material to consciousness. In the case of a young woman, a musician with numerous phobias and obsessions including stage fright, Ferenczi commanded her to perform for him. When the repressed tendencies became pleasurable, the activity was forbidden. This active treatment rendered fully conscious the long repressed infantile reminiscences. "In suitable cases psychic excitement can and must be shut off from unconscious paths of discharge in order by this 'rise of pressure' of energy to overcome the resistance of the censorship and of the 'resting excitation' by higher psychic systems" [p. 203].

Ferenczi compared active interference to the stimulating treatments employed in medicine for certain chronic processes. Acute exacerbation of a mucous catarrh not only leads to latent sources of the disease, but arouses resisting powers of the organism. Activity in therapy, he wrote, "effects an increase of the resistance since it stimulates the ego sensibility" [p. 213].

One of the points at which Ferenczi's active techniques coincides with modern psychoanalysis is in the use of the patient's contact function. According to Ferenczi, active therapy is indicated when the patient asks questions or, in modern terminology, when the patient makes a contact with the analyst. He was the first to note that when "the analyst counters with a question, [he] will direct the patient's interest to the source of his curiosity rather than satisfying him with an answer to the question" [p. 198]. Questions requesting aid in making a decision may be viewed as a means to interrupt progress in the analysis. Modern psychoanalysts view returning a question with a question as an aid in developing the narcissistic transference as well as a means of investigating the question and its underlying resistance.

While this approach to the patient's contact was a forerunner of modern psychoanalytic technique, Ferenczi differed from modern psychoanalysis in his understanding of illnesses such as schizophrenia. He concluded that schizophrenics, as well as certain other types, need the offer of love and encouragment from the analyst. "Too often they interpret neutrality on the part of the analyst as indifference and are, as a result, unable to work through their difficulties."

This and other theories of schizophrenia seem to us to place the analyst in an active position in determining the mode and timing of the interventions. Following the notion of contact function to its natural conclusion, modern analysts follow the patient's lead and work with these disorders according to one of Reich's (1949) original dictums: If the patient is left to his own determination of the amount and timing of interventions, the transference will unfold. The modern analyst intervenes by being neutral when the patient remains distant, and active when the patient asks directly for contact.

During early treatment, the narcissistic patient can utilize the only defense available to him: turning against the self, attacking the ego, or destroying the treatment. When the patient experiences a tense, non-feeling state, the analyst functions as an ego-syntonic object to minimize action until the negative narcissistic defense can be resolved. Object-oriented questions can create the atmosphere necessary while the defense is studied.

For the patient who has an insufficient barrier against external stimulation, the minimum feeding is provided by interventions timed to the patient's contact. This replaces the more threatening interventions timed to the therapist's own inner mechanisms. For the patient who is withdrawn and does not make contact with the analyst, several questions directed to neutral topics help the patient to maintain the defensive wall of narcissism so long as he needs it.

THE TREATMENT CONTRACT

Treatment begins with the first patient contact. Treatment-destructive resistances may be revealed in the first telephone call in which the prospective patient requests an appointment. The analyst investigates with the caller when he can come in and, if there is a time convenient for both, an appointment is arranged.

One resistant caller said that he would like a Tuesday evening appointment as that was his only free time. Though he expressed chagrin that nothing was available on that evening, he responded to the suggestion that he call again. The calls persisted for a number of months until a mutually convenient hour was found for the initial meeting. During the interview he revealed further resistances to paying and to time arrangements. In order to work with these resistances, it was agreed that meetings would be scheduled once monthly. He complained that it would take a long time to get anywhere, but since he insisted that he did not want to try anybody else, treatment began with the number of sessions he could afford, emotionally as well as financially. On occasion this patient pressed for additional hours, but on investigation it was revealed that he did not have a particular hour available.

He did not make these requests for more time during sessions but preferred to telephone. Usually it was suggested that he call the following day or week to see what would be available, but he failed to call at the suggested time. This man seemed to have anger so close to the surface that he was fearful of the treatment. The dialogue that ensued helped him to feel comfortable in expressing dissatisfaction and thus overcame his initial resistance to being there at all.

Contractual arrangements are made by mutual agreement. The habit of seeing patients three or four times a week grew up out of the early Freudian notion that we must convey our understanding of the patient's unconscious to him; therefore, the faster we get to understand him, the faster we can explain his problems and cure him. In practice, experience has demonstrated that patients do not get better faster because they come more frequently. Conversely, we have learned that greater frequency of sessions may lead to an intensification of the defense or a premature breakdown of necessary defenses, accompanied by further regression. Determining the correct number of sessions can best be done if the beginning patient is seen once weekly during a trial period during which time the optimal number of sessions may be established. When asked how often he would like to come, the patient may express a desire for frequent sessions, along with some external reason why it would be difficult for him to arrange that number. Joining this resistance, the analyst usually starts him at fewer sessions than he requests. After a few weeks or months, both patient and analyst may agree that greater frequency is desirable. The strength and flexibility of the patient's ego should determine this to the extent that the analyst's time permits. Arriving at the frequency of sessions is combined with an exploration of fees.

The patient's mode of interaction is investigated through the discussion of the terms of the patient contract. Compliance, defiance, and readiness for cooperation are investigated while fees and hours are discussed. The modern psychoanalyst will frequently ask a patient what he would like to pay. If a patient replies, "You're the doctor, you'll get what you want and I have to either take it or leave it," he has told the analyst something about his views on authority and his way of resisting submission. He can take it or leave it. The patient who replies to the question that he really would prefer to pay nothing, but is willing to pay whatever the analyst asks, has told the analyst that his dependency needs drive him to compliance.

When analyst and patient have agreed on treatment, on frequency of visits, a mutually convenient time, and a fee, the patient is invited to use the couch.

Students ask, "If the couch promotes regression, why put psychotics on the couch?" On the couch, regression is controlled by the amount of stimulation the patient is given. Basing the analyst's verbal communication on the patient's contacts tends to cut down the frustration. Conversely, sitting facing the analyst adds the unnecessary stimulation of visual contact.

In establishing a tentative diagnosis, we note that the patient was able to call for the appointment, learn the address, find the office, and arrive reasonably on time. If he can speak coherently, without fragmentation or confused states of mind, if he can state his reason for wanting treatment and can engage in cooperative interchanges on setting appointments and fees, little more need be discussed during the first hour.

In the first session, a patient may want the analyst to sum up, tell him what's wrong with him, how he is talking, or if he can be helped. On the other hand, he may want to know something about the analyst. He might ask, have you experience with this kind of problem? or what are your credentials? and/or can you help a person like me? It is undesirable in this early phase to give answers to these questions. First, it is not clear why the patient wants this information or how he intends to use it. Usually a question exploring his reason for seeking this information will reveal that he just wants to know how he is doing, feels that he should say something to the analyst, wants to learn if it's going to be a waste of time, or he cannot trust the analyst unless he finds out where he was trained.

If the patient is asked why he wants to know these things, he may reveal that he wants the analyst to give him information when he wants it. He may need to feel that he has come to an inferior person, and it might mean that the analyst is weak if the patient can get him to speak when he wants. If he fears that he may fall into the wrong hands, information about the analyst's credentials will not usually quell that fear. Questions about what the treatment can do or how long it will take cannot be answered, first, because we do not know, and second, because we want to explore the meaning of the question.

The patient's questions help the analyst to establish that the patient wants him to talk. The analyst's return of a question for a question explores what the patient would like the analyst to talk about. An ego-syntonic environment is achieved when the analyst is able to provide the proper amount and quality of communication, an amount experienced by the patient as neutral or accepting.

When the patient has agreed to come regularly and to talk, lateness may appear as a resistance. A new patient who wanted to come frequently described her financial difficulties as posing a problem and was invited to consider every other week. When offered this possibility, she decided she could come once weekly. At the second appointment she arrived twenty minutes late. The patient continued to come late and attacked herself for her inability to do better. An exploration of what the analyst could do to help resulted in further self-attack. "I can't change," the patient told her therapist. After consulting a supervisor, the therapist told her patient that it was all right, she didn't have to change. The therapist tried a new approach to the lateness. She thanked her patient for giving the analyst the time. Following this intervention the patient began to come five or fewer minutes late. This continued until the therapist announced her vacation, at which time the patient began to come twenty or thirty minutes late once again. This repetition was studied silently and this time no reference was made to the lateness and the patient returned to coming on time.

When does a patient come late? Usually when he has negative thoughts or feelings about the treatment that he does not wish to put into words. There is no point to resolving the resistance to coming late before its defensive function is fully understood. In the case just cited, the patient appeared anxious in the sessions and constantly in motion. Rather than bringing the lateness to the patient's attention, the analyst found that neutralizing the analytic sessions was called for first. The patient frequently turned around to look at the therapist. When asked about it, she said she wanted a response. She also revealed that she wanted to be met in the waiting room, rather than to walk in alone when the door was opened by the therapist. Questions about her preferences led to the expression of some of the thoughts that were causing her discomfort.

When the patient has feelings about the analyst that he is trying to hide or deny, he may describe these feelings in a relationship with someone else. In this case, the dissatisfactions can be studied silently, particularly as these complaints may relate to the analysis. There is no need to intervene except in response to a contact from the patient.

During the early interviews, while the analyst is investigating the dynamics of the case, it is usual to refrain from any confrontation. The analyst works to preserve a defense until he can establish that the patient can get along without it. The way that the patient perceives the situation—even if it be paranoid delusional—may represent the whole of that patient's perceptual field at the time. In order to increase a patient's orientation to reality, it may first be necessary to bring the existing field into the transference with sufficient intensity, long enough for new perceptions to be entertained side by side with the old. Then possibly the patient will be in a position to choose between the two fields (Spotnitz, 1969b).

A distortion of the perceptual field may be seen in the following example: A woman came for consultation and referral because the pressure of working for a family member had resulted in the growing conviction that she was the devil, or that the devil was getting into her. She was preoccupied with thoughts of this family member's potential death as well as a number of other fears. Her hateful impulses were experienced as alien; she experienced them as "not me." Thoughts that she was invaded by the devil whom she could not keep out fixed the responsibility for murderous impulses outside the "self."

In the early phase of treatment, regressive tendencies such as the above, are treated as a resistance to transference feelings. Until negative feelings can be expressed in the analytic relationship, the patient is trained to stay in the present. When the analyst is perceived as an ego-syntonic object, the patient is able to allow the unfolding of the narcissistic transference. Negative narcissistic transference resistance is aroused by pressure from the analyst for progress.

Even the analytic directive to talk must be viewed as resistance-provoking. Asking the patient to free associate is undesirable during the early phase of modern psychoanalysis. Hearing the content of what the patient says about himself is incidental to the treatment. Therefore, in response to the patient's questions, the analyst informs the patient that he may talk about anything he wishes. To the patient with an undifferentiated mental structure, the directive to talk about anything he wishes creates less resistance than the instruction to say everything.

Modern analysis, unlike classical analysis, does not focus on historical data. History is usually collected as it is volunteered by the patient. When the analyst follows the patient's lead, he does not intrude on the patient's ego (Spotnitz, 1969b). If a patient is asked why he is coming for treatment and he falls silent, the analyst may ask him to tell him a little about himself. If he begins to complain about his wife, then he has begun to tell his history as it is being relived. Asking a few questions related to the situation that the patient is presenting, rather than asking what he thinks and feels, precludes overstimulating the patient before having had time to evaluate his strengths and weaknesses. At the same time the analyst is conveying his interest and attention. One patient expressed his characterological fears when he said, "I know this is boring you. You must have heard these things a thousand times," or, "You must wish you didn't have to listen to me after hearing this kind of stuff all day." If, on the other hand, the patient talks uninterruptedly without reference to people for most of the session, the analyst may take an opportunity, when it presents itself, to ask a neutral question. The analyst need not disturb the patient about history unless it will serve some useful purpose in the treatment.

NEGATIVE NARCISSISTIC TRANSFERENCE

In modern psychoanalysis, resistances to the communication of the negative narcissistic transference are the first concern of the analyst. When the analyst has the impression that the patient is talking to himself or to the therapist as part of his mind, we speak of narcissistic transference. In a narcissistic state, instead of hating a frustrating object, the patient tries to blot it out. As we have shown, the defense used as a resistance is self-attack. The patient does not feel like talking, wants to run away, or feels that he is falling apart. The body feelings may be numbness, tenseness, or painful eyes. He sees no purpose in talking. He talks of suicide or self-mutilation. If these ideas are too frightening, he may say that he has nothing new to report or he may talk affectionately with reference to sexual fantasies, hinting a strong need for sexual satisfaction. In the negative narcissistic transference, the patient may say, "I loathe myself when I am frustrated." In the narcissistic transference resistance state, self-hatred may be concealed, and the patient may ignore the fact that the analyst is responsible for the frustration. In an object transference, a patient may say, "I'm holding back information because I don't trust you."

Early in the treatment the patient may tend to present more external resistances: a move to a new city, a job change with hours that interfere with his appointments, an illness that confines the patient to bed. The patient may take flight through missed appointments or coming late; he may sleep in sessions or remain out of contact. Certain patients will talk freely, chattering without saying anything. The modern analyst works to resolve those resistances that will destroy the treatment. The frustration of the treatment situation arouses aggression. Rather than verbalizing destructive thoughts, we have seen that the patient may resort to self-attack, or suicidal threats, or he may somatize. If no other defense works, he will leave treatment. Gradually through treatment the channels for action are cut off and the patient limits himself to words.

The withdrawal of object cathexis is used by the patient to defend against thoughts, feelings, and perceptions connected with the analyst. This defense is used to block awareness of early preoedipal states of the first few years of life when there was less differentiation of self and introject and when negative thoughts included sexual incorporation or annihilation of the object.

Two years may be required to study and work through a patient's variations of treatment-destructive behavior. Recurrences are expected, but if the analyst concentrates early on the verbalization of these tendencies, the pathways are established for communication.

The treatment may be preserved by controlling the degree of regression. To accomplish this the analyst may limit the number of sessions per week or limit the amount of silence to which the patient is exposed. To control the amount of stimulation, the modern analyst uses the patient's contact function as a guide. A student reported the case of a fifteen-year-old girl who was talking quite well but then said, "I have nothing to say." When she was told that she didn't have to say anything, she remained silent. The analyst asked her if she would like a topic suggested. The patient said yes. When asked what topic she would like, the patient expressed the feeling that the therapist seemed mixed up too. Then after a silence she asked if it was absolutely necessary to talk. When the therapist asked her if she would prefer to be quiet, she began to talk about the room. "It's too small," she complained. She didn't care for the pictures; they weren't very cheerful. She asked if it was necessary to stay in the room. The therapist asked if she'd like to stay. She said that her friend could leave whenever she wanted to. She reported then that she had to go to the bathroom. The therapist asked her if she'd like to go now. She said she'd wait. She could make it through the session. The patient was not given permission to act, but no commands were given. Following this patient's contact function proved to be effective in helping her control her behavior.

As the relationship is being established the patient is helped to gain control over his motility. Learning to discharge feelings in words can then replace self-directed aggression and acting on thoughts and feelings can be prevented. It is reassuring to a patient to be told, "It's all right to think and feel that way." When a patient jumps off the couch, the modern analyst may tell him that it is desirable that he remain on the couch. At other times, the analyst may join the patient by telling him that he doesn't have to use the couch now. If the analyst feels in tune with what the patient is saying and the patient says, "I don't want to talk to you," the correct response might be, "Why talk?"

After four months of severe treatment-resistance behavior on the part of one patient, the analyst expressed doubts similar to the patient's about continuing the treatment. At the following session the patient reported proudly that it was the first time he had made two sessions in a row. He said that he had had a dream about his mother, the first in which a woman in his dreams had a face. He figured it was the analyst in the dream since "You didn't throw me out for being a bad boy." He said that he had learned at an early age that he could not trust anyone with his feelings. "That's what I'm going through now," he reported. He said that last session he had wanted the analyst to know what was on his mind but had had a rush of thoughts and a fear that he would be incoherent (narcissistic transference resistance). "I felt accepted by you," he continued, "I always thought I didn't have any thoughts that were worthwhile." (This illustrates the preverbal ego at work.) "When I realize I don't have to do anything I don't want to, it releases me. I realized after last session that I wasn't talking about what was making me angry—your demands that I come to the sessions." (The analyst had become the demanding object.) "But to have someone care enough to get angry in a way that is accepting, that's a relief." (The analyst had now become the loving object.) In the first few years, the negative preverbal ego has few defenses at its disposal, so it must attack itself or destroy the treatment. A patient may experience closeness or oneness when the environment of the analytic session is viewed as ego-syntonic. It is desirable that the patient experience oneness if the lack of this experience was responsible for the fixation and if it will resolve the negative narcissistic transference resistance.

A patient who has been deprived of emotional closeness may act with the analyst as though he were alone in the room. He may even report that he feels he is talking to himself. It is possible to understand the isolation intellectually, but in order to respond, the analyst may have to join the patient's isolation, knowing it "as the patient knows it," so that the patient may learn to pull himself out of it. Insight cannot handle the memory images that are blocking growth if interchanges between the self and the object are at the stage of prefeeling, preverbal or preobject relations.

Answering the patient in kind is a modern psychoanalytic approach to the early resistances of the patient who is withdrawn in the session and for those who wish to engage us in philosophy. When the contact function of the patient is observed and responses are timed to the patient's communications, two things may happen: 1. The patient is more likely to receive the correct dosage of stimulation—being given neither too much nor too little—which balances the amount of frustration and gratification according to the dictates of the patient's request. 2. The patient is being trained to ask for what he wants. Since the narcissistic defense insulates the patient against unwanted feelings, interpretations of the defense, or of the patient's resentment of parents or of the analyst, his feeling of being forced to be in sessions, would only attack a necessary defense. In this phase of treatment the analyst wants to help the patient maintain his defenses while studying their role in his economy. Questions such as, "How can talking help?" may be answered with a similar communication, "It may not help."

If the early resistances are directed against the communication of transference feelings, the patient will want to talk but not be in emotional contact with the analyst. When the patient does make contact, the analyst may expect him to ask questions or make declarations which will reflect his current way of interacting. These contacts are studied, as well as the analyst's own emotional responses to them. With one situation, the analyst may feel flooded with ideas and theories rather than feelings. In other sessions, he may feel a great deal of sympathy, or a desire to talk and give factual information. He may wish to advise a patient or to prevent him from taking certain actions. All of these impulses to action are investigated silently by the analyst, as he would the patient's verbal and nonverbal communications.

Part of making a treatment plan is to decide the interventions which will resolve resistances and lead to growth. Questions put to a patient by the analyst may, though designed to be object-oriented, be framed in a negative and hurtful way when the patient is inducing unpleasant feelings in the analyst. It is important for the analyst to be aware of these reactions, particularly when treatment-destructive countertransference stimulates the analyst's desire to act.

In resolving resistance to the communication of transference feelings, the analyst first identifies the resistance used and studies how it is brought into the treatment. He is interested in what defenses the patient relies on and against what kinds of communication he uses them. Next the analyst investigates silently the relation between the repetition in the present and the patient's past experiences. And finally, he determines the interventions required to resolve the block to transference communications. Object transference resistance does not become a problem until the patient brings to the present situation a full repetition of past object relations. When the patient is ready to repeat the past in thoughts, words, and feelings without acting destructively, and the analyst is not acting on countertransference that would be detrimental to the patient, the patient is able to put the negative and positive transference feelings into words. In phase two of the modern psychoanalysis, these communications will be connected with memories as well as insight into the purpose that the resistance has served. Gradually, the channels for action are cut off and the patient limits himself to words.

If the patient is preoedipal and wants the breast, he may disguise his earlier needs behind sexual communications. One patient's descriptions of his sexual feelings were glowing reports, approaching rapture as it may be known at the breast. In his associations, he revealed a fear of being hated and his hatred of depriving females, revealing that he had suffered from a lack of emotional closeness when it was needed.

A student asked how growth is facilitated by the analyst when, in the narcissistic transference, the patient re-experiences the earliest prefeeling states in which the object was indistinguishable from the self. It would be difficult to find a patient who did not present residues from each psychosexual level, and we have found that, through echoing the patient's ego, the analyst presents the patient with an object with which he can achieve the emotional closeness needed for resolving resistance.

In a lecture given in 1920, Ferenczi (1950) observed a further resistance to analysis: countertransference as a result of the patient's influence on the doctor's unconscious feelings. Both Freud and Ferenczi noted that often the analyst appears abrupt and repellent toward the patient as a result of countertransference feelings. In these cases, both men were speaking of their fear of acting on positive countertransference feelings. A negative countertransference reaction occurs when the patient is in a treatment-destructive frame of mind. One of the first resistances seen in analysis—the resistance to the communication of transference feelings—is paralleled by the analyst's desire to get rid of the patient, or a tendency to forget the patient by either wandering off mentally during the session or having trouble remembering the patient's appointments.

Learning to provide the proper dosage of communication of the correct kind is the art of psychoanalysis. The following session demonstrates why it is important that negative transference be fully verbalized before the analyst conveys information or interpretations to a patient:

A patient complained that the analyst did not tell him the meaning of his dreams. He began his report of a dream, and every few sentences asked, "What does that mean?" If the analyst asked a question to which the patient responded with information, the analyst would then respond with information:

> The patient began his dream: I go to camp and I'm sitting at a table at the hotel. What does that mean? [Analyst: What kind of a table?] A dining room table. [Analyst:

Seated at the breast.] Four girls who are not at my table are high up in the hierarchy of the place. What does that mean? . . . [Ideal mothers.] One says, "You're going to go out with one of us." I have to go over to the two vulgar ones who compliment me on my looks. It reminded me of the way my mother used to show me off, commenting on how cute and well dressed I was. It is night time and I have to go to sleep. One of them tells me I have to make a choice. The only attractive one has already picked a guy I can't stand . . . . I chose the dark-haired one and in the next scene I'm sitting on a pedestal. They all come in. The brunette smiles at me submissively. I'm sitting up there like a king who's done his job. What does that mean? . . . [A child on his potty.]

Following the dream and the analyst's interpretations, the patient reported erotic thoughts about the analyst. These were presented not as thoughts and feelings, but as seductive communications. The patient experienced burning sensations in his eyes. He appeared unable to tolerate the gratification of his request being met, and in fact, demonstrated that the information had been over-stimulating. An intervention prohibiting seduction led to the admission that he wanted to avoid the pain and terror of aloneness, but he assumes the woman wants him sexually.

Helping the patient communicate preoedipal feelings is the job of the analyst. When the patient is attempting to cooperate, he will present these feelings in disguised form for the analyst's examination. Patients feel they should be "oedipal" and don't like the idea that they have preoedipal needs. (Neither do analysts!) To go back with the patient involves the re-arousal of the analyst's own preoedipal feelings as well as those of the patient.

In the following resistance to communication of negative transference feelings, the patient's longings are put forth first:

> I've been analyzing myself to try to determine why I sometimes feel out of it. It appears that I am in love with you and have sexual feelings for you which I shut out by self-absorption and fascination, to the general exclusion of others. I think that sometimes you try to encourage this love by smiling seductively at me. But, I'd rather have that than have you express hate to me. Anyway, I've done nothing hateful to you to deserve hate in return, but, unconsciously, I feel my sexual feelings for you are hostile and I more or less expect to be punished for simply feeling or thinking them.

A patient who is not able to express negative feelings directly is attempting to cooperate when he brings these feelings to the analyst disguised in dreams. An impulsive patient disguised his destructive impulse behind the wish to protect the analyst in the following dream:

> A seminar has been planned in which S. and K. are on one side of the debate against Dr. M. I arrive and find I'm the only one there on Dr. M.'s side. Suddenly, the debate turns into a baseball game and the opposition's centerfield is so far back he can't see to play. Dr. M. asks me to lend him my glasses but I refuse to do it. I think she's wrong. Why should I help the enemy to see? That would harm Dr. M.

This patient wants to keep his destructive self uninformed. Only in that way can he be protected from his impulses. He sought treatment from several analysts whom he attempted to set against each other. At a later period in treatment when trying to resolve who should be his analyst he provided the following dream:

> Dr. M. suggested that I go fishing. I am on a small island fishing (his analytic group). It is a beautiful place, but the weather is inclement—stormy and rain. I like it there. There is a woman there. She [or Dr. M.] suggested I seduce the woman. [He is in the group with his wife to resolve sexual and other marital difficulties.] I did not want to do this.

This dream reveals that if the patient continues to work on his marriage in the group he is in for stormy weather. He is conflicted about facing his feelings.

Another patient described her hostile impulsivity toward her children in a way indicating that there is no separation between self and introject. Speaking of her mother she said, "She is like a foreign body and I've always been aware I would not be able to protect my children from that 'her in me' any more than she was able to protect me from her."

We've talked about the relatively objectless state of narcissism in which the analyst may be experienced as a part of the self or as nonexistent. A patient may express amazement when he discovers objects and partial objects. One patient on entering the object world reported: "I went to my group and another patient addressed the analyst by name. Suddenly I had a feeling of the name. It was a real name. And there was a real person who went with that name. And he was really there—he existed and he wasn't me.

STATUS QUO RESISTANCES

An agitated patient who kept busy in order to defend himself against depression, reported fears of numbness and death during sessions and remembered waking up at two or three years old to find that no one was there. When the analysis is experienced positively by the narcissistic patient or when it offers him relief, he wishes to maintain the status quo. (This is transference used as a resistance.) If he is neither overstimulated nor deprived, he is able to maintain himself in treatment. While the analyst concentrates his attention on understanding and resolving resistances, meeting the patient's early maturational needs (for closeness, understanding, etc.) is an unconscious process in the analyst who is motivated to help his patient grow (Spotnitz, 1971-1975). Having the right feelings for the patient provides him with the emotional closeness that the preoedipal patient requires to move on to autonomy. The ability to feel the feelings induced by the patient is a function of the analyst's own mental health.

Working through the status quo resistance and observing the contact function of the patient, the analyst is able, silently, to increase his understanding of why the patient requires this degree of safety and comfort. When the patient demonstrates that he is not ready for more feelingful exhanges, his resistances are joined so that he does not experience the analyst as pressuring him to "grow up."

Usually the patient in this state is reluctant to express negative thoughts and feelings or to describe certain of his characteristics because he wants the analyst's acceptance and approval. When the patient reports that he is satisfied with his present situation and with his analysis, and denies having any negative thoughts, he is revealing his fear of the communication of negative feelings.

A man in the status quo phase reported frequently that he would like to see his analyst more often. Everything was going well. He described his wife as a lovely girl, his two boys as just wonderful. He appeared satisfied with things as they were, with the one exception that it would have been nice to see his analyst every day instead of twice a week. He appeared friendly, but vague and distant. His two ways of making contact were to ask, "Well what do you think about all this?" or, "When do you think you'll have more time for me?" After describing his business, he wanted to know if the analyst thought things were going well. Occasionally, he asked the analyst to sum up, but when asked what he would like to know, he continued talking about his work situation. At times when he was motivated to change, he described the omnipotent mother and attacked himself. "I can't feel disappointed in you. You do everything right. Disappointed in myself? Yes. You don't let me get close enough. I don't know why I hang on to these feelings of disappointment. I have always been disappointed in myself."

At such points, the analyst can reflect the patient's communications by devaluating the object, inquiring, "Why have I not been able to help you? You've done all the right things. You come, you pay, you talk."

As the patient begins to give up status quo resistances, he can express his transference feelings and thoughts more directly than in symptoms and actions. The analyst does not ask the patient to give up his resistances, but works instead to free the person from their compulsive use.

When a patient's characterological patterns have been brought in and developed into a narcissistic transference, "the analyst is in a position to loosen their compulsive grip" (Spotnitz, 1969b).

A woman with whom the analyst had never discussed treatment goals expressed disappointment in the analysis after approximately one hundred sessions. Although she was overweight, she never asked for help with this problem. She reported physical symptoms resulting from her excessive weight as impersonally as one would discuss the weather. In treatment, she demonstrated her aversion for any kind of frustration or discomfort. Later, the desire to maintain the status quo gave way to verbalized complaints. "I enjoy my food," she complained. "I can't give it up." Communications on this topic were repetitive discussions of diets, failures, and desire for more self-control, but no request for help. This woman was silently angry with the analyst for not curing her, but still could not verbalize her thoughts. In an exploration of an acting-out incident in which she "punished" the analyst, she first attacked herself and then, in response to joining, complained about her disappointment in the analysis. Until she had taken an action to "expose" the analyst, she was not able to verbalize. She was startled by her own behavior and this led to the direct expression of her transference feelings. At these points in the treatment, it is always the analyst's ability to continue the verbal exploration without interference from induced feelings that enables the patient to move ahead.

OBJECT TRANSFERENCE

In the middle phase of treatment, an object transference may predominate and serve as a resistance to remembering thoughts and feelings the patient had experienced for primary objects after he could distinguish between self and other. During this period, resistances to progressive communication and resistances to cooperative teamwork with a separate person interfere with the patient's ability to tell an emotionally significant story of his life. In this phase the patient experiences increased motivation to improve, but he fears new information. As the patient's resistances to expressing transference feelings are resolved, he verbalizes the repetitive patterns that were first brought in nonverbally.

A young woman who was neglected by her parents entered analysis feeling deprived and inadequate. Feelings were first acted out in the analyst's office. At the end of each session, she would linger at the door until she received a signal from the analyst that it was time to leave. As time went on, she responded less readily and lingered in a downcast pose. For many months she seemed depressed and apathetic, but she could not relate the condition to any life situation, including the analysis. When her behavior at the door was brought to her attention, she admitted she wanted to get all the time that she could. She expressed no further understanding of the behavior.

To reverse the pattern, the analyst began to be more casual about the time of beginning the sessions, fluctuating two or three minutes. The patient then began to glance at the clocks, checking one against the other, and checking these against her watch. All this was done silently. After a while she asked if the analyst had the time. Finally, she insisted that she was being cheated and demanded that she be given her due. No change occurred until she heard a lecture in which the analyst described the situation and the plan to resolve the resistance. Interpretations given in the office had had no effect. Insight emerged as a by-product of the connections established between impulses, feelings, and words. She described the resentment she had experienced, since the beginning of treatment, at the end of each hour when she was silently dismissed. The feeling was that she was just a patient who could only be seen for a fixed time. She felt cheated and deprived by the analyst. She explained that when she was angry, she felt provoked to steal time because it was the only way she would get anything.

This patient was demonstrating resistance to progress when, in a depressed state, she felt something was wrong and attacked herself rather than describe the object transference of, "You are a depriving person just like my mother." Acting rather than talking was her way of resisting progress. When the resistance gave way, she shouted, "You wouldn't give me the time of day." Transference began to give way to memory. However, the behavior continued through the exploration of the ego-syntonic character traits that lay behind her feelings and actions.

Transference feelings manifest themselves after the resolution of each resistance. Repeatedly, treatment-destructive resistances and status-quo resistances interfere with the communication of transference feelings. When they dominate, the analyst does not work for progressive communication. As these resistances are resolved the patient is moving towards the repetition in the transference of early object relations. We have seen that treatment-destructive behavior, resistance to the expression of transference feelings, is always given attention before any other resistance. When a positive narcissistic attachment has been formed, we have seen that the patient seeks the analyst's approval, and only with great difficulty relinquishes the enjoyment of a positive attachment. This period precedes a clear demarcation between self and primary object—the good feelings come from symbiosis with a powerful figure. When the patient is committed to using the analysis for emotional growth, he is ready to begin to know himself and his objects as he perceived them in infancy and early childhood. When the patient's narcissism has been successfully resolved in a narcissistic transference, the patient no longer attacks himself compulsively.

In the middle phase of treatment, the contact function of the patient is still the preferred basis for the analyst's interventions. When the patient, in a state of object transference, is working cooperatively with the analyst, he will respond to verbal feedings that arouse feelings of affection with direct expression of these affectionate feelings. When the object-oriented patient responds to verbal feeding from the analyst with feelings of affection which he then resists he will state: "I'm too embarrassed to tell you my feelings." He will respond to deprivation with the direct expression of negative feelings, stating: "I don't like this office. I don't like being here. I don't think you can help me. You don't even try." We have seen that when the narcissistic patient resists negative-object-transference communications when frustrated, he prefers to attack himself.

RESISTANCE TO TERMINATION

When the patient is faced with the termination of treatment, he begins to experience fears of giving up the relationship. He avoids these fears through a regression to and a revival of all the old defense patterns. The analyst uses the intervention of feeding back to the patient feelings that the analyst has experienced during the treatment. (The analyst could not return these feelings earlier when the narcissistic defense was the patient's sole way of relating.) What the analyst does with his induced (objective countertransference) feelings is the ultimate test of his ability to work for the emotional growth of his patients.

Both patient and analyst are bound in an emotional repetition of the past. To the extent that the repetition is of the patient's history rather than the analyst's, the feelings induced in the analyst are "the right feelings" for the patient's cure. The repetitive bind is resolved when both patient and analyst can feel the feelings, and prior to understanding, not act on them. When they can function together in the analytic situation with the proper feelings, emotional closeness is experienced by the patient. This is, of course, the *sine qua non* of cure with preoedipal patients. The patient begins to feel secure that the analyst will not act on negative or erotic feelings to the patient's detriment. Frequently patients report, "*The important thing is that you will be there to talk to me regardless of how you feel or what I say.*"

As the analyst becomes aware of his countertransference reactions, he begins to understand the interpersonal process between himself and the patient and, finally, the early interpersonal history that has led to the patient's repetition of feelings in the transference. The patient is freed by the analyst's understanding of their relationship to develop his own understanding of his experience. The analyst's impressions need not be conveyed to him in the form of interpretations since the patient, through the experience of emotional closeness and identification with the analyst, develops a desire to understand himself. Following this, he works cooperatively with the analyst to fit the pieces together. Usually the explorations originate with him following each working through of a transference resistance. (Resistance to teamwork.) Questions by the analyst about the patient's explanations will lead to further clarification. When there is a common understanding of a particular manifestation of transference resistance, the analyst's own emotional experience corroborates the patient's conclusions about his emotional life.

A CASE STUDY

ALMOST TWENTY YEARS AGO, a tall, attractive young woman appeared for the first time in the office of Dr. Meadow. She was twenty-one years old at the time of this interview. She demonstrated the bottled-up psyche which is characteristic of a person traumatized during the preverbal attempts to acquire the necessary maturational experiences for growth. She seemed physically tense and inhibited, somewhat sullen and accusing. She reported feeling controlled by others and said that this confused and frightened her. She said she would like to be in control of what happens to her. She wanted to be able to be with people without pretending or trying to live up to an image. She said she usually stays away from involvement because it is too difficult. "When I can't be perfect, I just go around all day trying to disappear." She added that in sexual relationships she was frigid, although she had repeatedly achieved orgasm in masturbation since the age of twelve.

She revealed that her first years had been spent in a midwestern city with a brother three years older, a mother who worked, and a father who was to leave their home when she was two-and-one-half years old.

She had almost total recall back to the time of her father's departure from the household. She remembered that she had always had an active fantasy life. In fact she spent many hours every day making up exchanges between two imaginary characters, bad Mary and good Carol. Mary teased and tormented Carol, who tried to think of ways to extricate herself. This early daydreaming was abandoned when at about five years old she began to listen to the Lone Ranger, a radio serial about a masked hero. The voice of the Lone Ranger came through an echo chamber which sent a chill down her spine when he asked the listener to return with him to yesteryear.

Her new fantasy expressed all her longings for an object she could love; all her fears were expressed in the dangers that befell him. Her rescue fantasies, in which she saved him from death and disaster, revealed her longing for mothering. With herself in the role of the good mother, life was tolerable. She described the fantasy in which she projected her own destructive impulses onto an environment that threatened the Lone Ranger, with her in the role of good mother to protect her mother from her pent-up rage.

Fantasies to cope with the loss of her father were threatened by the family's move to a new city shortly after she began school. This necessitated further psychic adjustments. Jane feared that teachers and classmates would know her thoughts and feelings. She wanted to be liked by teachers but could not tolerate them. She called them silly and dumb. The desire she expressed in treatment to be herself appeared to date back to this period when she had to hide her true feelings. Her mother remarried when she

was eight, and again she was interested in hiding how she
was feeling. The school and family adjustment combined
with the stresses of prepuberty led her into a more severe
depression, in which she gave up fantasy and began to
turn destructive urges against herself. Although she may
have appeared passive and apathetic earlier, her fantasies
had represented an internal activity and striving for mastery. From nine or ten on she appeared to have given up
the struggle and was blaming herself for an uncaring
environment. Her striving for perfection served two purposes: (1.) in fantasy it put her above and away from
others, and (2.) it was another way of saying, "I can shake
off bad thoughts and feelings."

TRANSFERENCE RESISTANCE

At first, Jane appeared disinterested in the events
going on around her. When required to cope with a real
situation, she experienced waves of danger. Analysis was
one more obstacle course. Her oral fear was of being
swallowed up: "You don't know who you are, you may
find out you're not real."

In the analysis she expressed her fear of being controlled: "I can't talk here because I'm expected to. You
want me to know everything." These expressions combined the fear of submission to the will of another, a fear
of incorporation, with the fear that she could not herself
control her impulses. She warned, "I'm afraid of excitement and of incest." She needed distance because over-
stimulation led to a loss of her sense of self. She fought
against emotional involvement with the analyst. (Resistance to transference.) Her first transference reactions

were negative narcissistic. She filled her sessions with self-recriminations and doubts and appeared unaware of the existence of another presence with her in the analytic room. At times she appeared physically rigid. The relationship-destructive behavior told the story of her life non-verbally: she slept through sessions, came late, and all else failing, resorted to silence. Money problems made it "touch-and-go" with respect to when the treatment would be terminated.

The first goal of treatment was to help her to be there in an atmosphere of minimal stimulation, to be able to stay for the entire session, and to tolerate the analyst's presence. The treating analyst, Dr. Meadow, had just finished control work with Dr. Theodor Reik and a seminar with Dr. Hyman Spotnitz, both of whom had prescribed a neutral environment with a slow-paced investigation of the material presented.

During this phase of the treatment, most of the analytic interventions were exploratory in nature, questions relating to external objects or situations in her life rather than about her thoughts and feelings. The theory was that ego-directed questions about her thoughts and feelings would be too much of a burden at that time. The few interpretations made were confrontations of a rudimentary kind, e.g. "There seems to be something about the situation that is frightening," or, "Could I be doing something that makes you want to stay away from the session?" Generally, the attempt was made to direct her to think about others rather than herself. A question regarding what the analyst may have done seemed to be at a safe distance from the ego, since it directed the thinking to an external object; at the same time, directing the attack to the analyst and causing the patient to think of the analyst as self-attacking, or, like her. As the patient directed more and more of her attacks onto others, the complaint that emerged most saliently was that she was expected to do something. She resented that others would ask her to perform when she should be left alone.

Responding to her when she addressed a comment to the analyst, described elsewhere as the contact function of the patient, or, during sessions when there was no contact, asking her only a few neutral questions on topics she was interested in discussing seemed to help Jane to learn to ask for what she wanted. In this non-stimulating environment, she began to feel less threatened and within a year, the more blatant treatment-destructive resistances, such as missed appointments, silences, etc., had been resolved. These problems appeared later whenever the analyst became ego-dystonic or provided an overstimulating or understimulating environment.

NEGATIVE NARCISSISTIC TRANSFERENCE

When Jane was able to arrive on time, she began to describe her transference feelings, but they were not the kind that indicated an awareness of a separate object. The analyst was beginning to be a twin image, representing to some extent early internalized object impressions, but impressions still confused with herself. In the unfolding narcissistic transference, Jane was consciously convinced that her treatment partner was wonderful, but she reported a sense of power after periods of silence, because "No one can force me to talk." At other times, self-attacks became a part of the transference communications when, complaining about her silences, she said, "Since I can't keep talking, there is no point in trying. I am a hopeless case." Her conversations were dialogues with internalized images. The emotional effect on the analyst in such sessions was to create a feeling of being in a void in which the analyst may drift off. As the analyst became aware of the feelings the patient's distance induced, she was able to understand and accept these feelings as a useful tool for understanding Jane.

As dependency needs came to the surface, Jane reported that no one cared. The anger that she directed against herself continued to fluctuate with periods of silence as a way of symbolizing the transference thoughts.

Continued investigations of her perceptions of the people in her real world encouraged her to examine the object field of her mind. She was asked if no demand should be made that she come to sessions. After all, why couldn't she come when she wished? One of the more effective interventions was made when the analyst, recalling a feeling Jane often induced, reflected her defense of self-attack by agreeing with her that she was really not doing too well. She was asked if she could help the analyst to understand why she was not doing a better job at helping her. This unleashed a barrage of abuse that such a demand would be made on her. It was the analyst's job.

This was one of the few interventions that moved her during this period. There was a secondary gain connected with keeping the analyst helpless to help her. She made it clear that the most important nonverbal communication she could receive was that the analyst had no vested interest in rushing her along. It seemed more important that she continue to view the situation as she did and put as much of it into words as possible, but that the analyst's behavior indicate to the observing part of her ego that she was not trying to influence her.*

Her requests for advice were investigated. Soon, she reported that her life on the outside was better, but that she was not getting along with the analyst in the sessions. This period culminated in a full session of silence, which was joined. It was not certain what meaning any intervention would have. At the next session she reported a sense of relief. She said she was afraid she would be forced to do what the analyst wanted her to do.

She began to present the negative narcissistic transference feelings in disguised form through dreams. The first dream reported that:

> My mother and I were roommates but I was to marry my brother. My mother and I were sitting very close and were looking at each other. I didn't like that. I thought, my mother is in the way of my marrying my brother.

Her associations were:

> I liked being with mother in the dream but was uncomfortable at the same time. The reason was I felt competitive with her and afraid mother would find out that she really didn't like me. I wanted her to like me. In the next dream I called you on the phone to say I couldn't come anymore. I had to go to a group meeting though I didn't want to. When I got there, everyone was sitting in a room with a big couch, chairs and a rug. I didn't recognize anyone. They were looking at pictures and paintings. I looked at one in which two people were walking up a hill and they were burning. I kept looking at it, but everyone

---

*This approach to joining has been described by Anna Freud (1946) and by Hyman Sptonitz (1969b).

else looked away. I thought they were being stupid. They told me I didn't belong there; it was only for people who couldn't look at those pictures. I went to the waiting room. You came in but we no longer had the same relationship. You were like a different person. You sat down beside me and I said something. You reminded me of a dancing teacher. She was young, pretty, and very sophisticated. I was afraid of her and you seemed like her. I was afraid I would not be accepted, that I couldn't fit in.

The sessions revealed that she was beginning to perceive the analyst as opposed to her awareness of the unconscious and feared she would never care for her. For several months she attacked the coldness and the uncaring attitude of the analyst. All that was repressed was the strength of her negative wishes. She talked about her fear of her own coldness and unresponsiveness to others, and particularly about the possibility she would always be frigid. Homosexual and incestuous feelings were reported alternately with feelings of isolation and separateness. She felt she might be endangering herself by telling the analyst these things.

POSITIVE NARCISSISTIC TRANSFERENCE

As Jane verbalized more freely, she began to think that what was making her so miserable was her hatred of others. She was moving from a desire to avoid contact, because of the pain, to an awareness of her longing for a benevolent and omnipotent mother. "You want for me what I want for me," she told the analyst as she began to experience more desire for contact. Her resistances were gradually directed against any thoughts or feelings that would upset the status quo. She was fearful that now that she had admitted her need, it was best not to feel angry with the analyst or to disagree with her. She asked the analyst's advice and wished to comply. The resistances that appeared as a projection of these feelings ("You don't want me to feel"), and the feeling that the analyst didn't care for her, surfaced from time to time, but the shift was taking place from distrustful watchfulness to the position "I will try to get your help." Of course, she wanted to lean on the analyst for the purpose of maintaining her regression. She did not think of herself as a separate person. As deprivation and hunger began to find expression, she became increasingly aware that because of the wall of narcissism, she had not learned to care for herself in fundamental ways. She made increasing contact in the form of requests for information and assistance of various kinds. The interventions that investigated her questions with questions were designed to foster narcissistic transference.

One theoretical position behind reflecting the patient's contact functioning is that the child's ego is strengthened when his feelings about how much stimulation he needs are respected. As children do not, in all periods of their development, need an understanding mother to provide them with answers, most patients do not need answers as much as an exploration of their resistances. This was corroborated by Jane's first object transference communications to the effect that she was special and she hated it—both her mother and her analyst treated her as special.

As the investigations increased in response to Jane's contact function, her communications revealed that she was closing the gap between the all-knowing analyst and the inadequate patient. The immediate result of the shift in her perception was the discharge of negative feelings regarding the loss of symbiosis with an omnipotent mother.

When she was alternating between narcissism and the acceptance of some emotional separation from the object, she shifted from the patient who complains each time that she must have a personal encounter, to the person who likes to make contacts. She began to experience some pleasure in others. This was the first characterological change. Jane began to move from the passive to the active position. In a joint interview with the man she was seeing, at a point when he threatened to leave, he complained of her lack of sexual responsiveness and the way it made him feel about himself. It is interesting that she was just beginning to be interested in remedying the problem.

She had reported at an earlier session:

> I've been considering our major problem and now I feel like it's getting worked out, although I still don't feel like letting go enough to have an orgasm. I don't want to have one. It's too frightening to keep maintaining it. I let it go. I prefer not to get so involved, although I do expect to have one eventually because I do get more involved. But it's too overpowering. There are too many unforeseen things that can happen, and I feel I'm going to give myself away or lose face or do something stupid, so having an orgasm is just too much, that's all.

Later, following their breakup, she resisted the expression of her anger and disappointment by a return to the negative narcissistic transference resistance–chronic complaining and the redirection of aggression against her own ego–the narcissistic defense. The repetition of her chronic passivity and demands to be fed, her attempts to remain passive and tied to a powerful figure, was understood intellectually by her, but she could not let go of it. Wanting marriage had increased her readiness for change, but the recent loss was a narcissistic blow that caused a temporary regression.

The technique that proved effective to deal with this persistent resistance was to reflect back her chronic coldness. In a dynamic fashion, the analyst confronted her with the feelings she had induced repeatedly during the early phase. She was asked how she could think that anyone could care for an unfeeling person like herself. Her reaction to this was one of immense relief. She reported that she was amazed that the analyst had so much feeling—so much feeling for her—that she had believed that she wasn't cared for because the analyst didn't reveal these feelings. She couldn't stand the knowledge that she herself was an unloving person; she wanted to be accepted despite it.

The result of this confrontation was to lower the defense against memories and feelings; she remembered what she had first experienced at the time of her parent's separation when she was two. Although the content of the ensuing sessions was not unusual, her appearance began to change. She appeared less rigid and frozen. The physical rigidity which had persisted throughout the first phase of treatment was replaced by a vivacity and animation. Now she appeared feminine. The explanation seemed to lie in her identification with the analyst's emotional response. * Her coldness had induced coldness in the analyst. Confronting her with emotion had given

* This effect was described by Nelson (1956) and Spotnitz (1963).

her an emotional image with which to identify. She reported that she had felt dead and that her mother wanted her dead. She related the loss of her lover to the earlier loss of her father at a time when she would have been discovering her limbs and mastering motility.

She connected her fear of dependency and the importance that passivity played in her life with her memory of being taken away on holiday by her father and the guilt she experienced because she wanted him to take her with him. She had mixed feelings, but the fact that any part of her wanted to be with him made her feel guilt about her mother. She produced a dream then in which her mother met a man Jane had been dating and said he was too fat. She related her early difficulties in coming to analysis to her fear that her mother would find out and disapprove of her coming. She also remembered how fearful she was that her lover would disapprove of her analyst, and that her analyst would not approve of her relationship with him. Among her other communications at this time was the feeling that she might be superior to her analyst, in dress, better taste in furnishings, and more intelligent. She feared that she would enjoy being superior. This appeared as a new way of maintaining distance in the transference. (Negative object transference.)

WORKING THROUGH

Negative object transference communications were resisted over a period of several years. It is not our intention here to review the periods of negative and positive object transference. The difference in functioning when the regressed patient begins to perceive reality is much more striking than in postverbal pathologies. This patient's style changed dramatically. She discovered that she could get many of the things she wanted. But once the idea of stopping treatment was introduced into communications, the earlier narcissistic defenses reappeared with striking force.

Modern analysts have learned to begin to mention termination long before the expected time since this helps to bring out the unresolved remnants of the narcissistic defense. In the process of working through these remnants, the analyst will find the history of his own induced countertransference feelings will be reawakened.

At a point when Jane seemed fairly successful in following her own orders and directing her life, the question of termination was raised. She had toyed with this idea from time to time but, when it was joined, her reaction was intense:

> You got me in over my head. Here I am trying to function
> as a normal person on the outside, doing all those things
> you got me to do. What I'm feeling angry about is that
> you made me do it all. It's just too much.

When the analyst joined her, she was asked why she couldn't have cut down on some of these activities. She flared up and asked why the analyst would get her into so much and then tell her just to drop it. It was the analyst's mistake and the analyst should take the blame for her being so burdened.

When asked why the analyst made her do it, she said, "You wanted me to have degrees and things. You wanted me to stop being a patient and start being a person. All I wanted to do was please you."

When it was mentioned that there was no hurry, she

said that she actually enjoyed everything she was doing but she got bogged down in resenting it.

She was still seeing her choices as remaining with the analyst in treatment and in a symbiosis, or having a loving relationship with someone else and leaving treatment. Having both was impossible. Working through duplicated the earlier unfolding of the narcissistic transference and transference resistances. We were both aware of a larger observing ego that could now put into words what she was experiencing.

In a session during which Jane recognized the resistance to expressing negative feelings, she remembered repetitive dreams in which she murdered someone. She was always relieved to awaken and find she hadn't.

> Now I realize I avoid negative feeling for you because I want you to help me. If I let you feel my negative feelings you wouldn't. I was not even aware I was avoiding them. I haven't known what I was doing since I was a little girl. People could trick me, use me, and I'd go right along with it like a dummy. I became rigid and dumb. Then people accused me of being cold. Anyone who caught my attention could lead me down the garden path. I felt helpless. Getting into trouble felt very exciting. I would expect others to take care of everything, to be more adult. Until I thought about those dreams of murder I never realized that about myself— that I like to get into dangerous situations because they are exciting. I never could figure out why you didn't throw me out. I guess it was the same reason as my mother's. It wasn't right and you wanted to do the right thing.
>
> [Analyst: I don't care about the right thing.] I knew that, but I look at it that you would treat me that way

because you do whatever you want to do. It was just a crazy way of looking at it. And I thought I had to do all these things because you wanted me to be like you, and I realized I'm not like you. That was hard to take. You kept me alive to be miserable. If you weren't just doing what was right maybe you're just interested in what others are all about. I happen to think that's pretty interesting too—an unfolding drama. If you're not doing this for moral reasons, maybe we are alike. I still can't think of you going through what I went through. You can't be like me.

[Analyst: Why couldn't we both appreciate life's drama and be different in other ways.] Well, we can, but your life experiences didn't push you beyond the pale whereas mine did. The only way I can make it without being dangerous is if I understand myself completely and have that as a base.I have to give up being so dumb.

Jane reiterated her desire that she and her analyst be alike and added that she always wanted her parents to get along. On an occasion when she attended a lecture where her analyst and another analyst were speakers, she said:

He was trying to shut you up. The differences of opinion have emotions connected with them. [Analyst: Certainly.] I don't like that. It's no fun. I feel much safer when you are getting along with him! It's better. It's not fun at all when you're not in agreement. Except for one thing. I'm so relieved to see that no one got killed.

At times Jane projected her desire for oneness onto her analyst. She also reported that she had never known anyone before. The analyst was the first object to enter her object field since the onset of her illness. The following session dealt with her transference feeling that the analyst did not want her to express her negative feelings.

> You want me to be silent in the same way that my mother had wanted me to be good. You never wanted me to have different opinions. I always felt there was something wrong with me. When I went to school, I looked bedraggled. My mother didn't seem to care what I looked like. If she didn't care, I'm not going to care.

In these communications during the session she spoke as though these events were occurring in the present. Having spoken about the past, she began to slip back into it. She continued in this state, describing how children teased her and she hated school. Then she returned to the present to express a transference resistance:

> There's really no answer to all of this. I'm just rehashing the same old story. We go over and over and over it, but it never figures out. She (Mother) made me feel I wasn't a part of her or the rest of the family and that is the way I have always felt.

For Jane neither choice was desirable. She could continue a feeling of isolation or she could cathect mother, family, and analyst. When she did the latter, she experienced herself as submerged, unable to have a separate self, to be different or to disagree. She said, "My mother wanted a dream person and I wanted to give it to her." Her perception of her situation when she attacked herself was that since she was not perfect, her mother could not be blamed for the way she treated her.

Jane fought against the belief that her mother hated her. When facing these fears she said, "I wouldn't have gotten into this if I could have believed what I knew. I was sure I must be misunderstanding her; that it must be my mistake, but I kept saying to myself, 'I don't know whether she likes me.' "

Jane began to sort out mother from self and to report memories of early narcissism. Earlier, "I," "you," and "me" were confused in her communications. The problem appeared to be that she had hidden her fear that her mother hated her and the hope she was wrong. Being told earlier by the analyst that she was a cold fish had a positive effect on her because it reflected her image of herself and because it meant that the analyst had some feeling for her. This helped her to verbalize self and early mother impressions.

In seeking autonomy Jane mistook what her mother wanted as her own will. In a more object-oriented phase, when she could distinguish internal self and object, she learned to project (in the true sense of projection of an internal object) onto the transference object while the self was kept intact.

CONCLUSION

In the early months of her treatment, Jane's objectless transference resistance and her need to avoid contact were expressed in treatment-destructive forms. She did not experience her negative feelings then, but seemed to have frozen them into the musculature.

Later she allowed the analyst to feed her symbolically, but maintained the status quo until reflection of her contact function had freed her to confront the analyst with direct emotional expressions of her deprivation in the analysis.

In phase two the loosening of the armor had resulted in a more spontaneous and vivacious approach to people, an increasing ability to see real objects and to actively seek satisfaction, with an increase in progressive communication.

When Jane was expressing herself more freely, she was able to explain her thoughts, feelings, and memories of the early treatment as well as of her early life.

EPILOGUE

Jane's own description of the first phase of treatment, a pre-ego state, objectless and unreal, was of one in which the analyst had no existence. Sometimes she experienced her analyst as part of herself. When she reported this, it corroborated the analyst's early experience with her in treatment. In the narcissistic countertransference, the analyst found herself experiencing the same feelings of objectlessness. As Jane began to experience her partner as real, the analyst began to have more regularly induced feelings that Jane had substance and was not a shadow. In reporting when she "came to life," Jane described the narcissistic state:

> In the first twenty years no one seemed real. As I began to realize that you were really out there, you became more and more important to me until I felt that you were the only real thing in my life. In fact, I even wanted to die. This was a big improvement over being dead. I thought I wanted to die, because it was so shameful to long for someone and so frightening to think someone might like me.
>
> I believed that because I *felt* the unreality, you would disappear. So then if you couldn't hang on to reality, and I couldn't, we would drift apart.

In summing up her treatment experience, Jane reported that most important of all was that the analyst overcame her desire to leave. This reflected her early fear of loss of control of her impulses. She remembered wanting to get away, "but you succeeded in getting me to stay instead of letting me run away. I guess I thought no one could stop me. I found you could." (Here she revealed that she felt she was an unwanted child.) "You gave me a new outlook. I got a different feeling about myself. I had always thought I didn't reach out because I didn't believe I really existed." (Here she expressed the perception that her mother had death wishes for her.) "When you made me stay, I thought you must believe I really exist. I had outer existence. That was the first step."

She described her negative narcissistic transference as follows:

> I never considered it a negative relationship because I had the same feeling for everybody. The positive aspect was that you made me stay. The negativism was very general, yet I always felt positive for everybody while I was wanting to get away, except for those occasions when I wanted to kill people for hurting me so much. Later, I knew I would keep coming despite my negativism which I still experienced as coming from the outside. [Her experience was that her mother hated her.] Everything seemed more real than what had happened to me before. When I taught myself how to type and got a good job, had a nice apartment, then went to college, I still felt like I was half a person. [Her complaint is that her mother had no positive feeling for her at birth.] Before that I felt like a zero. When he left me I wanted to die, and that wasn't unusual. When it passed, this time I felt stronger, whereas in the past it had weakened me.

Jane described the narcissistic defense as follows:

> I remember the first time I walked into your office–the
> only difference was you seemed to be behind a barrier
> which would never go away because of me. It was like
> looking at you through a glass. Now I don't see you
> through glass. Maybe I see you more clearly, more vividly.
> I blamed myself because I became cold. [Her narcissistic
> defense.] I thought my coldness was making you cold. I
> didn't want any warmth. I might have been complaining
> but I didn't want any. I must have thought I would melt
> (Laughs.) I think I just wanted to stay the way I was–
> frigid and cold and mean and dumb. [Her mother wanted
> her to take care of herself since she hated to take care of
> her.]

Jane revealed this thought when she said:

> I keep thinking I should be producing more, but that's a
> throwback. I used to think you thought it. But I thought
> it before I knew you. I think that you think that if I do
> things I'll feel better about myself, but that sounds like my
> mother. I didn't want to do anything and she knew it. I
> wanted to sit in my room and listen to the radio, look at
> pictures on the wall, be with my things and just read. I
> ended up doing it all her way but I still didn't want it.

THE RESISTANCE POTENTIAL
OF DREAMS

THE QUESTION HAS BEEN asked, "How are dreams used in modern psychoanalysis?" To begin to answer this, may we remind the reader that dreams existed long before psychoanalysis. Children and animals, who have no interest in psychoanalysis, nonetheless dream. But, Freud discovered that he had to consider dreams in treatment because his patients talked about them.

Patients still come in and talk about dreams, whether or not the analyst is interested. They tend to talk about all the things that are of interest to them. The analyst then becomes interested in understanding the patient's interest in these topics. Dreams can tell us what the patient wants, particularly what he wants to get out of analysis. We know from our experience that patients don't want to take the trouble of going through an analysis. One of the mistakes beginning analysts frequently make is in trying to help the patient get what he wants. If a patient feels he's gotten it, that usually ends the analysis, and the patient does not accomplish anything. Instead, the analyst tries to make it possible for the patient to stay in the analysis and to achieve a mature personality. To accomplish this, the analyst, recognizing that the patient has a conscious and unconscious, strives to undo the block to full communication. Ideally, the ego boundaries of the patient are extended to include the unconscious parts of the personality.

When the patient dreams, he may experience the dream as alien to his ego. He may experience it as something that just occurred, that just happened to him, and is not a part of him. As analysts, we want the patient to take the dreams that he produces and make them a part of himself. We want the patient to become aware that he is responsible for his own dreams and to recognize that they are a part of his own mind and personality.

The assumption is made that the manifest content of the dream is what the patient wants to create. As analysts we know that the manifest content of the dream is not usually a direct expression of the patient's wishes, that is, it is not an indication of what is consciously desired. However, since the purpose of the analysis is not just to correctly interpret the dream, the analyst reminds the patient that he created the dream, and that he is responsible for it. The patient is taught to accept responsibility for, and to understand his dreams, then to communicate what they mean.

If the patient gives interpretations of what the dream means which are discordant with the patient's behavior in general, the analyst may ask him how he knows the dream means what he says it means. If the psychoanalyst asks him what comes to his mind and he says, "I don't know," that may mean that he doesn't want to tell the analyst. The analyst doesn't expect the patient to know anything on the couch. All the analyst expects the patient to do is talk. On the other hand, if he says, "Well, I'm remembering my mother, father, grandfather," then the patient is cooperating. In other words, it is the patient's job to say whatever comes into his mind when the analyst calls his attention to the dream content. In this way the patient associates to his dream. Yet it must be remembered that the purpose is not to get the patient to say what the dream means, but to say everything he thinks in connection with the dream.

Patients usually begin analysis with dreams that are very unpleasant. In their dreams they are failures, or murderers, or their lives are in danger. The patient is aware of the terror he experiences, but not that he created the dream, or of the reasons he created the dream. One patient reported a first dream in which someone called her to come down the stairs, whereupon she discovered a casket. She was terrified when she saw that it was her body in the casket. The analyst suspected, and the patient eventually confirmed, that this was a very powerful suicidal wish. It took three years of analysis for the patient to be able to tell the analyst that her mother wanted her to die. This patient had no awareness of this perception at the time when she produced the dream. All she was aware of then was terror. She was not aware that this dream represented her wish to please her mother by dying for her. Interpreting this dream at the time it was presented might have precipitated a suicidal attempt. By resolving the resistance to communication the analyst was successful in helping the patient to tell the analyst what the analyst had suspected from the beginning.

As the patient lies on the couch with the analyst out of view and the room dim and quiet, the maximum stimulation he experiences comes from the internal organs of the body, as it does in sleep. Psychoanalysis is a setting patterned after this dream-like state of sleep in which motor output is limited. During sessions, the primary output from the motor neurons and the spinal stem is speech. In sleep, the unconscious communication is the internal stimulus that produces the images and the words of the dream. In sessions, through the creation of a dream-like setting, we hope that the patient will convey to us his unconscious wishes in the transference situation. The unconscious wishes are first presented in disguised ways and later in the transference. In the dream, as in other material in the session, the patient uses words and images that are disguised communications. The patient has something to tell the analyst and a resistance to telling it.

We might ask why the patient doesn't tell the analyst directly what he has in mind in the first session. When he reports a dream, why doesn't he tell what the wish is that he is producing in the dream? Of course the answer is that dreams, as other behavior, serve the dual function of permitting the patient to report material he would like to get to know (to cooperate with the analyst) and to avoid knowing by disguising the meaning (use the dreams as a resistance). When he disguises his wishes, the patient reveals a conflict between the part of him that wants to communicate and the part of him that wants to hide. The patterns that the patient uses to defend himself in dreams are similar to the defenses and disguises which he uses in the analytic situation. When awake, instead of giving his thoughts and feelings, the patient will tend to get into positions of tension, to engage in inappropriate behavior, to repeat himself, or to communicate in such a way as to make it difficult for the analyst to understand him and the meaning of his symbolic communication.

In the early part of an analysis it is not necessary for the patient to understand what lies behind the disguise or how he defends himself. A simple analogy is, if a person knows what is wrong with the car, it isn't necessarily going to help the car to run properly. The best solution is to have a mechanic fix it. Ignorance in analysis is like general anesthesia; if the patient doesn't know what's going on, the analyst can operate successfully with a minimum amount of intervention, for the analyst need only deal with the unconscious resistance. If the patient is aware of the process, the analyst may have to deal, additionally, with conscious resistance. The key to the unconscious resistance, we have found, is the dream. Dreams help the analyst predict what the patient is going to do in the transference relationship. In the analysis of the girl who dreamed she was in a casket, the analyst could predict that she would try to prove that the analyst wanted to bury her. Through the dream, the analyst was provided with the opportunity to know what the patient intended to do and to study the situation. He could predict what would occur in the transference.

The analytic situation is studied from the moment the patient arrives until he leaves. The analyst studies how the patient functions, the meaning of his behavior, his thoughts and feelings and memories, trying to discover the dominant resistance at work at a given time. When the resistance is understood, the analyst makes a plan for resolving that resistance. He uses the dreams, all the reported material, and the patient's behavior to get the patient to give up his resistance and directly report his transference feelings. To do this, the analyst first helps the patient use his dreams as a resistance. The analyst conveys to the patient the desirability that he dream. Patients may then resist by not dreaming, they may produce nothing but dreams, or they may produce dreams in which they fail. These failure dreams reveal aggression. If a patient were to come in with a dream that he was hungry and in the dream be fed, the analyst would know the dream was mostly positive; but, most adults do not have such direct wish-fulfillment dreams. These are more often the dreams of children.

Their dreams are easier to understand than those of adults. A child will dream he has an ice cream cone, is licking it and enjoying it, or he will dream he asks for an ice cream cone, is refused it, and cries all night, thereby expressing a reaction to his disappointment at not receiving the ice cream cone. Children use dreams to describe what they would like to get, or their resentment about what they did not get. But later, as a result of the development of the ego and superego, dreams are disguised. Children's dreams and the dreams of psychotics are relatively undisguised because their egos are relatively undeveloped and the individual is relatively free to become aware of his unconscious wishes. The older and more experienced we become, the more we realize that our polymorphous perverse, and our destructive wishes, are socially undesirable. So that when they come into play in the course of sleep, as adults, we try to disguise them.

For example, the little girl's dream of asking her father for an ice cream cone while they are out in the park, and receiving it, is reflecting her wish that she receive the ice cream cone, which she did not receive in reality during the day. Asking for ice cream in the park was in itself a disguise. What she was asking for, on the deeper level, was milk and affection from her mother. And she was also asking for affection from her father. She accepted the no, then went home and dreamed of satisfaction because she had received a great deal of affection from her mother and her father. In the dream, the ice cream cone symbolized the quest for the breast. The breast symbolized her quest for affection. Her father's refusal reminded the child of her disappointment at not being able to continue breast feeding and bottle feeding.

In adults the need for maternal affection is disguised in sophisticated forms of nourishment. Whatever is ingested, however, does not satisfy the need. Adult eating does not compare with the pleasures of breast or bottle feeding. Alcoholics will tell you that they take to the bottle as a way of recapturing the aura of pleasure when they were receiving the bottle. The need to disguise is the need to be grown up and to hide the fact that we still want to enjoy infantile pleasures. Because adults want the admiration of the people around them, they try to keep their thoughts and feelings operating on an adult level. This is done to win social approval as well as self-approval.

The modern analyst uses dreams in connection with current material being discussed in the analytic session. Dreams presented in treatment are investigated as a source of information on the unconscious and on the ways in which the patient defends himself. A very good example of how the dream can be used was the analysis of a patient who came into treatment because she was having a great deal of difficulty with her husband. She had had many years of analysis with many analysts. This was a woman whose conscious mind was cooperative. She was never late, she talked freely, and she paid her bills regularly. In the analysis it was the dream that revealed the truth about her transference feelings.

Before the analysis began the patient said she was afraid to come because she was afraid the analyst would insist on preserving her marriage. The analyst made it clear that he would not influence her unless she made a direct request. The plan to observe her contact function was followed. The analyst proceeded by speaking to her only when she asked him to, only answering questions she wanted answered, and only trying to influence her in ways she wanted to be influenced. This was very important in her case because, as she subsequently reported, she felt that she had always been threatened by her husband and by her other analysts. Her dreams confirmed this. Many times in her life she had had dreams of being raped or attacked by being choked and she couldn't say a word, but would wake up in great terror.

As she became more and more convinced in the present analysis that she could control the analyst, her dreams changed character. Instead of being raped and attacked and unable to utter a word in her defense, she had dreams in which she was being attacked but she was able to cry out in terror and ask for help. Still later her dreams changed and she was no longer being attacked, but people were trying to seduce her and get to her.

Eventually she became interested in developing relationships with men and women that would be mutually pleasant for her and for them. In connection with this material it became clear that the need to be raped and squelched and to not say a word was symbolic of her relationship with her mother, who had completely dominated her, and later, her relationship with her father, who had been a tyrannical person. She actually felt at that time that she was part of her mother and that anything her mother requested, she had to carry out. Her husband, at one time, came to represent her mother. Any wish he had–especially to rape her–she had to submit to. She had to go into analysis, she said, because she felt she was dying, being squelched, and she felt she would have to commit suicide.

The dreams revealed that she was being suffocated in the marriage and couldn't even utter a word in her defense. As she was able to influence the analyst and assert herself with the analyst, she began to be able to control herself with her husband and her children so that their relationship improved. She became a person who could assert herself and hold up her end of the marriage. She had been threatened because she had unconscious needs to submit completely to her husband, be completely dominated by him, and at the same time project this to him as his desire and his wish, which she completely opposed.

When the analyst recognized through the dream that the patient was going to try to get him to bury her, he structured the analysis in such a way that the patient knew he would not intervene unless she wished it. She argued that the analyst was acting so that he could use her for his own benefit. Slowly it dawned on her that the analyst was not out to "do her in." With understanding of the transference meaning of the dream several lines of exploration suggested themselves. The patient was asked why the analyst should do the things she was accusing him of. This type of joining technique does not challenge the patient's perception, but merely pursues it.

Dreams can be of great value in resolving the patient's resistances to describing his negative attitudes. Patients have a need to disguise their hostile wishes toward the analyst or toward their parents. Frequently a patient can present in a dream a hostile feeling that he cannot express directly. The following dream was produced by a patient who had never expressed negative feelings for his analyst or group analyst. To the contrary he was flooded with admiration for them.

> We [patient and analyst] were crawling through a tunnel together. You [analyst] had insisted that we had to go through the park to get to the office. We came to the tunnel and the tunnel was too low so I was instructed to get down on my stomach and crawl through and pull my bicycle through with me. This was a very unpleasant experience. I was very upset. In the next segment of the dream I went to my group analyst, and I wanted to tell him what a rotten experience it had been. But when I got there, the group analyst was sitting in a corner talking with some other people and ignoring me. In the third segment of the dream I was on a bus. When I got on the bus, I saw my former therapist. He was very friendly and we had a wonderful chat and when I got off the bus, at the last minute I thought of something I wanted to say to this therapist.

"Why was it," this patient asked the analyst, "that I waited till I was getting off the bus to tell that man the things I wanted to tell him?" The message this patient is conveying to his analyst is his feeling that if he had worked to tell him [parents] all the things he should have said, he never would have had to be stuck with the present analyst and that group analyst. This was a cooperative dream. The patient was bringing in and presenting clearly his feelings.

Sometimes patients disguise their feelings in the manifest dream to win the approval of the analyst. When there are incestuous feelings or desires to annihilate the analyst, who is seen as a rotten person, or as a threat to the patient, the patient really doesn't want to tell this. When he has these thoughts, the manifest dream content usually combines the wish with the defense against the wish. In most adult dreams there is a conflict—a conflict between the patient's wish and his defenses against that wish.

Frequently a dream tells us a patient wants to act out negative feelings by leaving treatment rather than by putting the feelings into words. Through his symbolic communications the patient gives the analyst the opportunity to understand his treatment-destructive resistance. If a patient feels understood, he does not leave analysis and does not want to, but if he cannot speak comfortably to the analyst, some resistance is not resolved. Many times the patient is interested in proving the analyst is doing an ineffective job, and that he is a worthless analyst. That attitude on the part of the patient does not help the analyst to cure the patient, particularly if the patient acts on these feelings. If the patient is becoming more and more hostile to the analyst, the analyst may understand why, if he understands the patient's dreams.

One patient repetitively reported dissatisfaction with his relationships without saying anything new. He simply reported that people were difficult to get along with. Occasionally, he complained about the analyst. In one particular session, a dream was remembered in the middle of the session and was told as an association to the topic the patient was already discussing. Just before reporting the dream, he had a fantasy. It occurred to him that he could get on his motor bike and ride off on a cross-country tour. He imagined himself riding down the street on his glorious bike while people by the roadside admired him and exclaimed, "Oh what a lovely sight."

In the dream I was at my girlfriend's house, and there were a lot of people there that I didn't like, but there was one person whom I did like, and that was an old college friend. This old college friend was someone who had, in our college days, been very helpful to me and very protective. And I thought that I would like to take my friend out of the house, for two reasons: To take him out and show him my motorcycle which was parked out front. I felt that my bike was unique and I wanted my friend to admire this bike. The other reason was that I was very uncomfortable being in a house with all those people I didn't like. This was a good way to get away from it. So we went out of the house to look at the bike. When we got out there, the bike didn't look the way I wanted it to. And I was a little disappointed; in fact, this reminded me in the dream, of how it goes in the sessions with you. I intend to really show you what an interesting person I am, but when I get to the session I am disappointed because I do not measure up in performance to what I expect of myself.

Based on the dream and his associations to the dream, we understand that the patient is in conflict between living with people, on the one hand, and being a wonderfully admired object on stage on the other. In other words, this patient expressed a desire to run away from treatment. To run away means to be admired from a distance. To stay means to think of himself as a disappointing person and to tolerate people who don't appreciate him. The patient is warning the analyst that unless some of the rage can be redirected away from the self, he cannot tolerate the burden of the transference feelings.

When the patient presents a dream, there is an opportunity for the analyst to understand the dream and then to get the patient to talk about it. If the analyst misunderstands the dream, the patient is not going to tell him about it. It is important to be in tune with the patient, and to know what the dream means, in order to get the patient to tell the meaning of the dream. The basic principle is that everything the patient does from the moment he arrives in the analyst's office is an association to the dream. However, we have recognized that verbal associations may serve a resistant function since they represent what the patient knows consciously and pre-consciously. The dream itself is a product of his whole personality and can tell us more about that personality. If the patient's total personality is understood, his behavior on the couch should reflect the symbolic communication of the dream and the dream associations.

In dreams a patient may report that he is falling apart—he may be dying, he may have cancer. Or a patient may report a confused state of mind in a dream. This may be presented without mention of transference feelings. If the patient tells us in a dream that he is in a precancer state, it is a good idea to believe him. If he says he is in a prepsychotic state, it is a good idea to believe him. But many patients will not come in and tell us directly what is wrong with them. They will give a dream in which they go crazy, as a warning that you, as the analyst, had better shape up soon, or they are going to go crazy. When a patient cannot communicate directly, he may come in with a disguised cancer, a disguised psychosis, or a disguised attempt to leave the treatment. The associations may continue the disguise of the dream thoughts. The message is: if it continues to be this tough here, I may disappear, begin to somatize, or develop a psychosis. In the disguised form, the patient will let us know what he wants us to know. Sometimes a patient cannot tell us either in his associations or in his dreams, what he is planning, or how he plans to put it into effect, what somatic illness he is going to develop or what treatment-destructive behavior he is going to display. Then the difficulty is in reading between the lines. If we understand the material as a whole, using the dreams as a part of the total presentation, it will be easier to get in touch with what the patient is telling us about his plans. He wants us to know, he wants us to investigate, he wants us to be interested in resolving his problems, so that he will not have to develop cancer or a psychosis.

Dreams help resolve a patient's resistance to describing positive wishes as well. Focusing on the disguises used by the patient and why he uses them makes it possible for the patient to recognize his positive wishes. The disguised negative and positive wishes can be investigated by the modern psychoanalyst and the resistance to these can be resolved. The proof that it has been done successfully is the patient's report of the negative and positive wishes in adult and mature language. The primary problem in working with dreams is to resolve those disguises that the patient uses to conceal his negative and positive wishes. When these are investigated and successfully resolved, the patient will produce the material that he was hiding in his dreams. If one understands that the importance of resolving resistance lies in helping the patient learn to state his transference thoughts in less disguised form, then one understands how to work with dreams in modern psychoanalysis.

Frequently one is confronted with dreams themselves used as a resistance. If the patient comes in and reports dream after dream, that he cannot make any sense out of the dreams and does not get any message from them, it is important for the analyst to recognize that the patient may be using an overwhelming quantity of dreams to resist the analyst. This particular resistance can be resolved frequently by asking the patient what memories are connected with the dream rather than by asking the meaning of the dream. Some patients like to go into great detail on the meaning of the manifest content of the dream. When patients bring in excessive numbers of dreams it is of no value to the analyst unless the patient can be helped to give his associations to those dreams, and the associations preferably should be memories of emotional significance in the life of the patient.

As the patient becomes more cooperative with the analyst, his dreams become clearer and less disguised. The more acceptable his wishes become to him, the more often he is able to bring in less disguised wishes. The cooperative patient gives visual images of early preoedipal experiences. When the symbolic communication drops out, the patient can then describe the previously disguised communication in mature language. Dreams dealing with preverbal wishes communicate wishes that the person cannot communicate in any other form because his power of recall has been lost. The patient's thoughts have nothing to do with these preverbal experiences which were either very frightening or met with severe disapproval.

The following dream, reported by a cooperative patient, reveals that she feels in danger. At the same time she assures the analyst she will protect them even though it is the analyst's fault they are in danger.

> I am rowing in a small pond. There is someone in the boat
> with me who grabs me and lunges and the boat is in

danger. Now I pick up the oars, but do not understand why the person did this. I start to row. The person with me does not know how to swim, but I do. I felt that I had to row to a safe place and put the person out and then go on about my business and do what I had to do.

This is a dream in which the patient is with a person who really isn't very competent, and through clumsiness and awkwardness really endangers her own life as well as the patient's life. By producing this dream the patient reveals her fear that the situation is precarious. She did, in her associations, say: "I really think that I dream these things so that I'll be careful not to present you with anything in the session that you can't cope with." What the patient means by this is that she does not want to tell the analyst directly that she would like to ground the analyst for arousing fears of her hostile wishes. The patient is also reporting two parts of herself and her desire to be rid of the dangerous part.

In the case of an obese woman, the patient never asked the analyst for anything. This was her characterological response. In the sessions and in her dreams, she behaved as she believed the analyst wished that she would—that is, not be any trouble. In her dreams, this patient goes to banquets. In one dream, she went to a banquet and tried to reach for the food, and the food moved away from her. She just could not reach it. She had another similar dream in which, for one reason or another, she did not eat. In the dreams, finally, she denied herself food. During that session she said that she did not want to eat. She is convinced that the analyst wants her to lose weight and her dream confirms this belief. This patient, in her dreams, is behaving like a "good girl."

If a patient produces a dream in which she is behaving

in a way to win the analyst's approval, and then reports in the dream that this is what the analyst wants, but the analyst is interested in the patient achieving what the patient wants, his mode of intervention will be governed by the strength of the patient's belief. If the patient is strongly convinced that the analyst wants this, then the analyst will not usually question the transference, but will investigate without challenge to the patient's perception. The question then might be put to the patient: Why is she doing what the analyst wants instead of pleasing herself? If, on the other hand, the patient comes to the session with a dream in which he reports that the analyst wants something, but he is not sure he is reading the analyst correctly, he reports, "It's not right for you to want that. You do want me to do that, don't you?" The patient thus raises the question of whether the analyst does or does not really want him to behave this way. His perception of reality is on a little better ground. He is not one hundred per cent convinced that his perception is correct, since he himself has a question about it. The analyst might then ask him what evidence there is for his perception or how the analyst has given him that impression.

When the analyst becomes aware of the dream as a transference resistance, he also becomes aware of the value of resistance. When the resistant content of a dream is understood, various parts of the personality are able to communicate with each other and the patient is able to communicate with the analyst.

We might ask a patient how he feels about his dreams. We might ask him why he produced a dream; we might ask a patient what the meaning of the dream was. We might use any of these if it would resolve a resistance. It is not necessary to investigate a dream in a session. However, the dream may be utilized in the session in many ways.

In modern psychoanalysis the analyst also studies his own productions to understand the patient, carefully analyzing reactions induced by the patient and reactions based on the analyst's needs. An analyst may produce a dream which, when understood, helps him to get in touch with countertransference feelings that were preventing him from resolving a transference resistance.

The following case was originally reported (Spotnitz, 1963) in abbreviated form. The student analyst produced her original notes for this account; they demonstrate how the analyst, by resisting making a necessary intervention, may prevent the patient's progress. The student reported the following session with a young male patient in a state of negative narcissistic transference. The patient is describing his feelings about his wife's trying to push him into getting a better job.

> She talks about it every day. If I have to put up with this much longer, I'll divorce her. I should get angry, but I can't. I feel angry and miserable about taking so long here to grow up. I feel like taking a knife and plunging it into my head. (This is a narcissistic defense.)
>
> Analyst: Why don't you do it?
>
> Patient: No, I'm not going to do it. I want to grow up. That's what I'm coming here for.
>
> [Next Session] The patient says he is starting a job to-morrow. He is afraid he won't have the right attitude and then he is liable not to work hard and he'll get fired and then he'll go downhill and be a bum and he'll *have* to shoot himself.
>
> Analyst: What's wrong with that? (Again the analyst is joining the narcissistic defense.)

Patient: I feel you are trying to destroy me, wanting me to kill myself.

Analyst: *I don't want you to kill yourself. I just want you to say what comes into your mind.*

Patient: Well, I don't want to die. I get mad at myself because I'm not doing enough.

The analyst's first dream took place that night. In this dream her patient repeated his statement: "I think you are trying to destroy me." Then he got off the couch and stood before her. "I was terrified that he would kill me," she said. That ended the dream. Associating to this dream the analyst said that instead of reporting to her patient that she did not want him to kill himself she might have asked him what difference killing himself could make when he was destroying himself anyhow. She felt he then could have vigorously denied the self-destructive impulse and verbalized the feeling. The student analyst had felt that following through in that way would be difficult for her because she could not be so hostile. She understood his standing up in the dream to signify that he intended to attack her sexually.

The next night she had a second dream about the patient. "In the midst of a session," she reported, "a stranger walked in and my patient left the office with him. The stranger returned alone and tried to rape me. I cried for help but no one heard me. I woke up in a state of terror." The second dream indicated to her that she actually wanted to be raped by someone other than the patient.

Through the understanding of her dreams, the analyst was freed to use her negative, narcissistic countertransference feelings in the next session with the patient.

A week later, after analysis of the analyst's dreams, the patient said he felt hopeless. There was nothing to do but kill himself.

> Analyst: Why don't you do that now?
>
> Patient: I think of that as painful.
>
> Analyst: You could die without any pain.
>
> Patient: I don't want to die.
>
> Analyst: Why can't you die to please me? (This questions his tendency to protect the analyst.)
>
> Patient: I don't want to please you. When my wife nags me about getting a better job, I feel like not getting a job just to spite her. I get mad when you talk about my dying. How would you like it if I picked up the table and smashed it over your head? Would you like to die then?

Eventually the analyst recognized that her difficulty in responding to her patient in harmony with induced feelings of anger was linked with her own unmet needs.

Freud was the first dream interpreter of scientific merit. The development of the concept of transference resistance taught analysts a new approach—the analyst does not interpret dreams to the patient. The purpose of analysis is not to interpret dreams unless a patient's resistance will be resolved by telling him something. The patient's contact function tells us when this is so. If the analyst is working with the patient to help him to impart his memories, thoughts, and feelings, intervening for that purpose is then the proper use of dreams.

In general, the dream is treated as a part of the total session, rather than as an independent unit. The analyst may ask the patient why he produced the dream, what ideas he has about the dream and its meaning; all the ideas he has then become his associations to the dream.

When the analyst can help the patient to say everything, the patient becomes healthier and better adjusted. If the patient is willing to come to the session and tell the analyst his dreams but the analyst cannot resolve his resistance to saying everything, then the patient fails in the analysis. When the analyst knows how to use dreams in order to resolve resistance, they can be used for purposes of analysis.

Some patients say that as the analysis proceeded, they never felt so bad in their lives. Everything went from bad to worse when they had expected analysis would make them feel better. The analysis does not work to make the patient feel better or worse. The purpose of the analytic experience is to help the patient feel all his feelings and put them all into language. We know that many patients, if they have a potential for unhappy feelings, do experience them during the course of analysis. If they were fortunate and had a very happy life, with good parents and a good background, analysis could be limited to a very joyful, happy experience with the analyst. But since no one has had such an experience, analysis will lead to many unhappy moments. One girl who was born prematurely cried for a whole year after she entered analysis. After a year the analyst asked her why she had been crying for a whole year, and she said, "I was born prematurely, I couldn't cry for the first year of my life. I have to make up for it."

Originally, Freud studied dreams because he wanted to know what they meant. Today psychoanalysts are fairly well agreed on what dreams mean. They are usually an attempt on the part of the individual to express a wish, a wish disguised by the defenses of that individual. In analysis, a patient lying on the couch finds ways to avoid telling things. It is the analyst's job to have the patient tell everything and tell it in mature language. This will include the meaning of his dreams. The patient tells the analyst about his dreams not only through language but through symbols. When a patient reports a dream, the analyst accepts this disguised communication. If a patient has contempt for the analyst and shows it by not removing his hat on arrival, the analyst will want to have some understanding of why the person is doing this and will help the patient to tell him why. The same principle applies to the dream. The patient is trying to tell the analyst something in a disguised way. It is not important to find out what the patient is trying to say. The important thing is to resolve the patient's resistance to telling it without disguise in mature adult language.

When practicing dream interpretation, Freud used dreams to find out what the patient was hiding. As modern psychoanalysts we want to know why he is hiding and why he is using these various methods to hide.

Telling the meaning of the dream to the patient may show the patient what a wonderful dream interpreter the analyst is or how successful he was in understanding the dream, but it does not resolve the patient's resistance to direct communication. If the analyst is working with his patient to help him interpret his memories, thoughts, and feelings, intervening to explain his dreams for that purpose is the proper use of dreams.

SPECIAL RESISTANCES IN
GROUP ANALYSIS

P ROGRESS TOWARD greater specificity in group treatment has been retarded by the lack of distinction in
the field between the group approaches that are
designed to provide the patient with the type of experience he needs to become a healthy and mature personality,
and those group approaches that are addressed to the
needs that have only an immediate gratification value.
Every procedure needs to be evaluated in these terms: does
it primarily offer a gratifying experience or one that will
help a patient outgrow his emotional immaturities?

The fact is that most group treatment today is an-
chored to the values reported by the pioneers in the field.
Perhaps their first outstanding discovery was that the
shared treatment experience facilitated socialization. Patients were observed to establish meaningful contacts in
the group and, after testing out new modes of relating to
others, went on from there to social groups. Contributions to ego functioning and superego relaxation were
pointed out as other benefits. The family configuration of
the therapy group and the reaction to the therapist as a

parental figure were found to facilitate the reliving of the oedipal situation. It was observed that suffering and symptoms were alleviated more rapidly in the group than in individual treatment. The support and attention of other patients and the discovery that they had similar emotional problems were among other benefits reported.

Much group treatment today is oriented toward goals consonant with these values, being conducted by and large to reduce the symptomatology, to help socialize, to provide cathartic release, and other benefits of a superficial nature.

For the analyst who is to help people become more effectively functioning individuals, whatever their problems and stage of life, group therapy is unquestionably a powerful mode of treatment, perhaps the most powerful we possess, though not necessarily the best for all patients.

One aspect of effective group treatment that has received little recognition is the exposure of patients to feelings that catalyze growth processes. The more serious the patient's problems, the greater the need for the feelings that would facilitate desirable changes in behavior. One major advantage of group psychoanalysis is that the need for feelings can be met in the treatment setting itself. Analytic group process equips the analyst with a powerful resistance solvent he does not have in the dyadic relationship. Beside monologue and dialogue, there is the groupalogue. The emotional impact of spontaneous reactions of the group members and the criticisms and suggestions they volunteer make group discussion a potent factor in the resolution of individual resistances.

Anyone who can arouse all the necessary feelings in his patients has little need to expose them to a therapeutic group. But it would be difficult to find an analyst who has such a broad range of feelings available. Moreoever, should he confront patients with feelings that are "manufactured" for a therapeutic purpose at hand, they will be rejected as a worthless substitute. Unfortunately, much of the emotional feeding that patients engage in when left to their own devices is either damaging or, at best, unproductive in terms of personality growth.

Despite their unconscious tendency to feed one another emotionally, patients cannot be expected to obtain the precise feelings each of them needs if the analyst operates on the principle of laissez-faire. Because of the toxic elements in the feelings at the patients' disposal, the analyst must tap the potential source of emotional nourishment in such a way as to discourage destructive emotional interchange and to facilitate the communication of emotions that are conducive to desirable changes in behavior. When tendencies to engage in damaging interchanges are observed, the analyst may intervene appropriately to head them off.

The crucial factor in any type of psychoanalysis appears to be the unlearning of those pathogenic patterns of defense that have become part of the patient's character structure. These patterns must be freed of their charge so that more desirable defenses may come into function. When the symptomatic patterns are analyzed and dealt with effectively as resistance, they are gradually modified and outgrown. This enables the patient to respond more appropriately to the environmental pressures.

If the analyst maintains a climate that will stimulate the members of the group to contribute to the resolution of pathogenic patterns in their fellow group members, the group process will prove constructive in modifying these patterns.

Patients tend, in the group environment to call attention to the resistant attitudes and behavior of their co-patients when they differ from their own modes of functioning in the group. The tendency of group members to deal with each other's resistances is fostered by educating them to work well together as a unit and by responding appropriately to the total picture.

It is through resistance that a person undergoing psychoanalysis communicates the information that he is unable to engage consistently in spontaneous, emotionally significant verbal communication. The notion of resistance as the absence of communication and the antithesis of self-revelation has been discarded in psychoanalysis. Resistance is now conceptualized as the primitive, inadequate, indirect form of self-revelation characteristic of a person who functions on a level of emotional immaturity.

Resistances in the group may be seen as the voluntary and involuntary methods by which group members avoid giving, or helping co-patients to give, a spontaneous and emotionally significant account of past and present psychic realities, feelings, and thoughts in the immediate situation.

The resistance pattern of a group member may operate in relation to the therapist alone, to one or more co-members, or to the group as a whole. It is the presence of common or group patterns in addition to the individual resistances which accounts in large measure for the more complex nature of analytic group process. Psychoanalysts now tend to focus on the group patterns and to intervene primarily to deal with them. The familiar conceptual tools of analytic process, transference and resistance, are used to resolve the group resistance to effective functioning. By concentrating on the group patterns that become a resistance to constructive interchange, the analyst works for the reactivation and working through of the obstacles to maturation. He controls the transference and regression as he concentrates on these group patterns of resistance. The analyst's skill in enlisting the cooperation of the group members in dealing with each other's resistances usually spells the success or failure of his effort to promote personality growth through a shared treatment experience.

Attempts to overcome resistance forcibly are undesirable. Resistance performs a communication function, telling us something about the patient, provided, of course, that someone is present to decipher the meaning. Protracted silences or idle chatter are two patterns used when a member wants to hide, be ignored, or avoid attack. These patterns become special problems in the group when other group members cooperate in the maintenance of these resistances. Discovery of the message being concealed by the resistant behavior is the key to the resolution of these problems, but rather than attempt to abolish the resistance, the group analyst accepts it as an expression of the character of the person.

THE MONOPOLIZER

Although the compulsive talker is usually seen first in individual analysis, he can be handled by a skilled analyst in a group that has reached an advanced stage of treatment. Needless to say, the analyst should be expert in the management of mobilized aggression in the group situation.

The patient may communicate that he is talking on and on because he doesn't want to tell anything. The monopolizer often clings to one idea, or rambles on through subjects that are unrelated to his fundamental emotional problems. Consonant with the general theory of dealing with resistance is that though the monopolistic pattern interferes with analytic group process, its presence should initiate the silent study of why and how it was activated in the immediate situation, and also an investigation of its historical significance in the patient's life. On the basis of analysis, the therapist decides what to do about the monopoly. Before intervening verbally in any way, he explores such questions as the following: Should the resistance be silently tolerated in the present situation? Should it be encouraged, even supported, because it serves a useful purpose? Should it be discouraged because it blocks therapeutic process?

If the monopolizer is usurping time and attention that his co-patients really want, the hostile tone of the groupalogue will make that clear. If they become destructive in their reactions, the analyst intervenes. Frequently, however, the insights inculcated through group discussion provide sufficient protection so that the monopolizer is not exposed to antitherapeutic attack. The group's understanding or interest in influencing him in a constructive way to function cooperatively usually prevents him from becoming the target for scapegoating.

If the groupalogue indicates that the monopoly has the support of the other members of the group, the analyst deals with it, not as an individual resistance, but rather as a group resistance expressing itself in diverse but interlocking patterns of behavior. In other words, the overtalkative patient and other members who encourage him through their prolonged silence are recognized as engaged in a combined operation. The special advantage of this approach is that no member of the group is neglected during the exploratory process. Each of the silent members may be asked why he is trying to escape being the center of attention.

But it may then become clear that the patients who have been maintaining silence really want to talk. In that case, the group analyst asks what has been blocking them from helping the monopolizer to stop talking, and from verbalizing their own desires to talk. If the obstacle to asserting themselves is a lack of understanding, the analyst may formulate his communications with a view to ascertaining what has been motivating the monopoly and their own unwilling silence. If the monopolizer responds to the various approaches that have been described, the analyst does not have to institute special interventions.

The main danger is that the monopolizer may arouse so much hostility that the group will be disrupted, or the monopolizer either eliminated or irreversibly damaged by the reaction of his co-patients to his behavior. The nature and degree of damage that can be caused by verbal hostility are variable; their assessment is a matter of careful judgment. The patient who arouses intense hostility among other group members may be temporarily traumatized through the experience of serving repeatedly as a psychological punching bag. Usually this damage is more than compensated for by the contribution that such experiences make to the process of desensitizing him to the impact of negative emotions and helping him to become a more resilient personality. It is important, however, to bear in mind the possibility and danger of irreversible damage. While the assessment of damage from verbal hostility is a matter of judgment, no leeway can be extended to the discharge of negative feelings in motor action. Any patient who cannot adequately control his behavior in a therapy group does not belong there.

In instances in which the patient is not sufficiently influenced by the group exchange to give up the monopoly, the analyst may have to address himself to the problem more deliberately.

If the monopolizer is utilizing a relatively mild resistance of the oedipal type, this will usually respond to interpretation. For example, a group member may state, "I've been quiet here a long time. You'll have to listen to me for a change." Or the oedipal pattern may be used by more than two members; they may jointly announce that they intend to manage the group, or refuse to allow their fellow patients to take the stage during the session. Such individual and subgroup patterns would also be interpreted as much as possible in terms of the immediate configuration of total behavior. While the resisters would be helped to understand why they were trying to prevent others from talking, or usurping the parental role, the other members would be asked why they permitted themselves to be treated as children. The monopolies just illustrated are involuntary and unconscious patterns, but not compulsive.

Preoedipal patterns of resistance are rarely responsive to interpretive procedures. Reflective techniques and emotional communications are generally employed to help the monopolizer function more cooperatively. When the behavior is joined or psychologically reflected, the patient is helped to give up a pattern outside personality control without experiencing undesirable pressures or narcissistic mortification.

For example, the analyst may say to a group member who has been talking uninterruptedly for fifteen minutes, "You have been talking for fifteen minutes today and nobody has interrupted you. Shall I ask the others if they object to your talking another fifteen minutes?" The analyst may say, "Since you have talked for fifteen minutes, everyone else has the right to talk the same length of time without being interrupted. Wouldn't you like to take over, John?" More forcefully, the analyst may say to another member, "Would you like to talk for fifteen minutes and give him a taste of his own medicine?"

The analyst may respond with an emotional communication. For example, talking for the same length of time in a tone of voice similar to that of the monopolizer.

Another approach would be to inform the resistant patient that, after talking so long, he now has to remain silent for the rest of the session. Should he attempt to capture attention again, other members will usually tell him, outright, that they don't want to hear from him.

Usually, however, the analyst does not have to engage himself in such procedures because the group members respond emotionally to the monopolizer on their own initiative.

Another individual resistance that meets with attack and then yields to understanding is monopoly by interruption. For example, a woman who maintained silence about a variety of traumatic events going on at the time in her own life, characteristically cut in on group members who were communicating their own problems. Identifying herself with one of the problems being presented, she would say, "The same thing happened to me," and proceed to talk at length about a more or less comparable problem she had encountered in the past. She was a brilliant woman with a sparkling sense of humor; hence, the group's response tended to play into the resistance. Even the member who had been interrupted rarely raised an objection and, at times, the monopoly was encouraged by requests for further details or advice. The first step taken to resolve this pattern was to help the woman become aware of what she was doing. Her fellow patients asked her questions about it.

As in this case, the pattern of monopolizing by interruption often originates in sibling rivalry. This woman revealed that she had developed this pattern in childhood to cope with a sister who was the preferred child in the family. The patient had identified with her sister's problems in order to strengthen her marginal hold on, and to gain more securely, her mother's attention. After she discovered that she could receive the desired audience in the group by discussing her own problems, she gradually learned to control the impulse to cut in on the others in the group with a "me too."

Feedback from group members makes a tremendous contribution to the resolution of resistance patterns that interfere with the therapeutic process. Negative feedback has the effect of inhibiting the overtalkative member. Postive feedback stimulates a too silent member to function more cooperatively.

THE SILENT MEMBER

When one member of a group tends to remain silent, the analyst questions silently: Does the group consciously wish him to be silent and are the others abetting him in this behavior? If it becomes clear that the others are helping him maintain silence, there are four different types of interpretation that may be indicated. It may be pointed out that the silent member is being treated like a sacrificial lamb for the selfish purposes of the other members; that they are helping a frightened little baby escape becoming the center of attention; that they are expressing their own desire to be silent through his silence; or that they are combining with him in a sado-masochistic operation.

On the other hand, it may be decided that the others really want the silent member to talk. In that case, it is desirable to know what blocks them from helping him to talk. If the blocking is caused by their lack of under-standing, the analyst may provide it.

The group members need to be educated to the idea that there is an appropriate way to withhold information, as well as an inappropriate way. The inappropriate way is to clamp one's mouth shut, like a baby trying to fight a bottle his mother is trying to put in his mouth. An older child can open his mouth and explain that he isn't hungry, or is not eating carrots because he is holding out for chocolates. The group members who have something to say and can't say it in the group at that time are expected to emulate the behavior of the older children. The appropriate way to withhold the information is to explain why it is being withheld. For example, the patient might say that he has something on his mind that is too painful to talk about, or that it might be to his disadvan-tage to talk about; or he may say that he cannot trust the group with this information.

This resistance may require joining before the patient is able to give it up. For example, demonstrating to the patient by explanation or illustration that he has the right to withhold information may resolve the resistance. This entails silence and respect for the group member's privacy and for the confidential nature of his communications. When a patient learns through the group experience that an explanation (verbal) of his withholding of information is more effective and comfortable than total silence, this is also advantageous to the group analyst because it is easier for him to deal with the more mature pattern—either to help the patient preserve it or to help him give it up if he so wishes. Therefore, one tries to determine the reason for the silence. A resistance that is supported because it makes sense may or may not be resolved later. In a therapeutic group climate, the objections to the disclosure are eventually resolved and the resistance melts away.

It is not usual procedure to apply any available technique in a routine way. Interventions will not be effective in dealing with resistance unless they are based on the recognition of the specific factors associated with the silence of the patient in a particular group setting. Any short-circuiting of the process of understanding the patient is apt to get the analyst into trouble. One always has to begin with understanding. This takes much longer than intervening by rote, but it assures the continued presence and favorable personality development of a problem patient who might otherwise have withdrawn from the group.

It would be going too far to say that "resistant" silence is never motivated by a desire, whether conscious or unconscious, to provoke hatred or resentment. There *are* people who are fearful of being overwhelmed by positive feelings and fight against being liked by other group members. This is notably true of schizophrenic patients who find a loving atmosphere difficult to tolerate.

Nevertheless, silence stemming from a fear of being liked or an actual wish to be disliked is rarely encountered.

In one group, protracted and general silences constituted the outstanding resistance during the initial stage of the treatment. When the group members recognized that their silence was acceptable, they started, one after another, to talk about various life experiences and feelings. They recognized, eventually, that a strong wish to be liked by the others had operated as a block to meaningful communication. This wish, coupled with a fear that they would make disclosures that would be disapproved of by their co-members is a common source of resistance in the therapy group.

Some very dependent people are unable to express their negative feelings out of fear of the consequences. They resist verbalizing resentments because they do not want to run the risk of being further humiliated. They cannot tolerate a fear of loss of self-esteem. Fears of losing desirable contacts with other human beings and of being exposed to undesirable contacts appear to dominate their behavior.

Each patient tends to identify his co-patients with significant figures in his past and to relate to them with a strong emotional charge. The presence of additional transference objects endows resistance with a multidirectional character; that is, it operates not only in relation to the analyst but also toward one or more fellow patients. It may also operate toward the group as a unit. Classically, the group activates early attitudes toward the family, wherein patients tend to view the group as mother. Frequently, they relate to the analyst as a parent and to their co-patients as siblings competing for his attention. At other times a group member may be seen as a parent.

To illustrate these processes, a middle-aged, self-absorbed spinster oscillated early in group treatment between two patterns often observed in highly narcissistic patients. She either maintained silence while the other patients conversed, or seized on their silences as a signal to plunge into a lengthy, lifeless monologue on an inconsequential topic. She talked rapidly, disjointedly, and in such a low monotone that it was difficult to hear her, let alone make sense of what she said. The verbal barrage helped her to conceal her actual thoughts and feelings.

This pattern had originated in her attempts, at the age of four, to prevent her mother from finding out that she engaged in sex play with other little girls. Her incessant chattering prevented her mother from asking questions about how she had been spending her time. Just as her mother would have censured her had she revealed the truth, this patient anticipated disapproval and criticism from the group if she disclosed her emotional problems. This was an unfortunate problem to be saddled with because it gained her the reverse of what she wanted—hostility instead of favorable attention and admiration. Her co-patients responded with impatience, annoyance, and agitation. They told her that she was dull, uninteresting, and incoherent, and was wasting their time bringing up matters about which they could not care less. She was always hurt by these comments; at times she cried. Failing to recognize that they were trying to help her function cooperatively, she would complain that they had no feeling for her and then she would refuse to talk. Eventually the other group members recognized that her verbal barrages communicated a great need for affectionate attention.

When she retreated into silence, on the other hand, she was encouraged to join in the groupalogue. When she talked about what she really thought and felt, she was helped to continue. Her perceptive comments on problems of other patients were warmly received; she was told that she was helpful, sympathetic, and understanding. They, in turn, then demonstrated genuine interest in discussing the problems she disclosed. She thus discovered that she was better able to get the attention she craved when she did not try to conceal her need for it. Occasionally, when she felt frightened and insecure, she reverted to the original patterns, but they ceased to be compulsive operations.

CONCLUSIONS

The monopolizer is chiefly a problem because democratic sharing of time and attention is regarded as desirable in group treatment. What is sought is versatility in talking rather than time sharing on a strictly mathematical basis session after session. Sometimes the monopolizer facilitates versatility in talking, and sometimes he interferes with it. The monopolizer may interfere with the democratic sharing of time and attention; moreover, he may corner the precious psychological commodities mentioned to engage in communications that are repetitive in substance and disguised in meaning. By provoking hostility among the other group members, however, the monopolizer eventually facilitates group communication. Patients who were disinclined to talk earlier join the resistance, and in so doing, they compete with the monopolizer for time and attention. Each competitor, in turn, produces others, and the monopolizer is gradually cut down to doing no more than his share of the talking.

Thanks to the presence of the monopolizer, one is rarely confronted with periods of silence in the group sessions. Group silences usually terrify the beginning analyst. More than one student has reported that he didn't know how to get the group started until a patient began to talk and so provoked the group that the other members told him to shut up, and they took over. Even the experienced analyst is not very happy with group silences. Consequently, the monopolizer performs worthwhile services for the analyst who wants to provide patients with an emotional group experience and to eliminate protracted silences in group sessions.

The role of the modern group analyst is to resolve resistances to communication. To do this he must create the climate in which group members can experience feelings and engage in constructive emotional communication. Since we recognize that patients enter the group in different stages of emotional immaturity, it is helpful to formulate the goal of the treatment as the emergence of the emotionally mature personality, and this is the goal toward which the modern psychoanalyst works.

BIBLIOGRAPHY

Abraham, K. (1966), *On Character and Libido Development*. New York: Norton.

Adler, Alfred (1908), The aggressive drive in life and neuroses. Germany: *Fortschritte des Medizin*. No. 19, July.

Aichhorn, A. (1948), *Wayward Youth*. New York: Viking Press.

Alexander, F. (1961), *The Scope of Psychoanalysis*. New York: Basic Books.

Arieti, S. (1961), Introductory notes on the psychoanalytic psychotherapy of schizophrenics. In: *Psychotherapy of the Psychoses*, ed. A. Burton. New York: Basic Books.

Bak, R. C. (1939), Regression of ego orientation and libido in schizophrenia. *Int. J. of Psychoanal.*, 20:

———.(1954), The schizophrenic defense against aggression. *Int. J. of Psychoanal.*, 35: 129-134.

Balint, Michael (1952), New beginning and the paranoid and the depressive syndromes. *Int. J. of Psychoanal.*, 33: 214-224.

———. (1953), *Primary Love and Psychoanalytic Technique*. New York: Liveright.

———. (1959), Regression in the analytic situation. In: *Thrills and Regression*. New York: Int. Univ. Press.

———. (1968), *The Basic Fault*. London: Tavistock Publ.

Bender, L. A. (1955), Twenty years of clinical research on schizophrenic children with special reference to those under six years of age. In: *Emotional Problems of Early Childhood*, ed. G. Caplan. New York: Basic Books.

Bergler, E. (1958), *Psychoanalysis and the Writer*. New York: Basic Books.

Bergman, P. & Escalona, S. (1949), Unusual sensitivities in very young children. In: *Psc. St. C.,* 3-4: 333-352. New York: Int. Univ. Press.

Bernstein, Arnold (1962), Introduction. In: *Paradigmatic Approaches to Psychoanalysis*, ed. Marie Coleman Nelson. New York: Psychol. Dept., Stuyvesant Polyclinic.

Binswanger, L. (1957), *Sigmund Freud: Reminiscences of a Friendship*. New York: Grune & Stratton.

Bion, W. R. (1962), *Learning from Experience*. New York: Basic Books.

Bjerre, P. (1911), Zur radikalbehandlung der chromschen paranoia (Radical treatment of chronic paranoia). *Jehrbuch Fuer Psychoanal. Forsch.*, 3: 795-847.

Bloch, D. (1965), Feelings that kill: The effect of the wish for infanticide in neurotic depression. *Psychoanal. Rev.*, 52: 51-66.

Bowlby, J. (1966), *Maternal Care and Mental Health and Deprivation of Maternal Care*. New York: Schocken.

Boyer, L. B. & Giovacchini, P. L. (1967), *Psychoanalytic Treatment of Characterological and Schizophrenic Disorders*. New York: Science House.

Brill, A. A. (1949), *Basic Principles of Psychoanalysis*. New York: Doubleday.

Brody, S. (1963), Simultaneous psychotherapy of married couples. In: *Current Psychiatric Therapies*, ed. J. Masserman, Vol. 3. New York: Grune & Stratton.

Brunswik, E. (1956), *Perception and the Representative Design of Psychological Experiments*. Calif.: Univ. of Calif. Press.

Bullard, D. M. (1960), Psychotherapy of paranoid patients. *Arch. Gen. Psychiat.*, 2: 137-141.

Campbell, J. (1949), *The Hero with a Thousand Faces*. New York: Pantheon Books, Inc., for Bollingen Foundation, Inc.

Cohn, Franz (1940), Practical approach to the problem of narcissistic neuroses. *Psychoanal. Quart.,* 9:64-79.

Clark, L. P. (1926), The fantasy method of analyzing narcissistic neuroses. *Psychoanal. Rev.*, 13: 225-239.

Clevans, E. (1957), The fear of a schizophrenic man. *Psychoanal.*, 5 (4): 58-67.

Eissler, K. R. (1953), The effect of the structure of the ego on psychoanalytic technique. *J. Amer. Psychoanal. Ass'n.*, 1: 104-143.

———. (1957), Remarks on some variations in psychoanalytic technique. *Int. J. Psychoanal.* 39: 222-229.

Escalona, S. (1940), Effect of success and failure on the level of aspiration in manic depressive psychosis. *Univ. Io. Stud. Child Wlfr.* 16: 197-302.

———. (1953). Emotional Development in the The First Year of Life. In Senn, Milton, *Problems of Infancy and Childhood.*(Transactions of the Sixth [1952] Conference). Josiah Macy, Jr. Foundation, Ann Arbor, Michigan,

———. (1974), Activity and passivity: Influences of maternal style on early ego development. Unpublished paper presented at the Second William Menaker Memorial Lecture: New York University Postdoctoral Program, Jan.

———. (1974), Unpublished letter to Phyllis W. Meadow. Spring.

———. & Heifer, G. M. (1959), *Prediction and Outcome: A Study in Child Development*. New York: Basic Books.

———. & Leitch, M. (1949), The reaction of infants to stress. In: *Psa. St. C.*, 3-4: 121-140. New York: Int. Univ. Press.

———. & Sears, R. R.; Wise, G. W.; Benjamin, J. D. (1949),

Approaches to a dynamic theory of development. Round Table discussion. *Ops* 1950, 20: 123-160, discussion 157-160.

Ezriel, H. (1956), Experimentation within the psychoanalytic session. *Br. J. Phil of Sci.*, 7: 29-48.

Federn, P. (1952), *Ego Psychology and the Psychoses*. New York: Basic Books.

Feldman, Y. (1958), A casework approach toward understanding parents of emotionally disturbed children. *Soc. Work J.*, July.

Fenichel, O. (1945), *The Psychoanalytic Theory of Neurosis*. New York: Norton.

Ferenczi, S. (1950), *Selected Papers of Sandor Ferenczi*. New York: Basic Books.

Fine, R. (1962), *Freud: A Critical Re-Evaluation of His Theories*. New York: David McKay.

Flournoy, H., (1927). A Report on a Case of Folie à Deux. *Swiss Archives of Neurology and Psychiatry*, Vol. 20, pp. 44-55. Discussion by Charles Ladame, pp. 331-337, 1927.

Flugel, J. C. (1970), *Man, Morals and Society*. New York: Int. Univ. Press.

Freeman, Lucy (1972), *The Story of Anna O*. New York: Walker & Co.

Freeman, T. (1963), The concept of narcissism in schizophrenic states. *Int. J. Psychoanal*. 44: 293-303.

Freud, A. (1946), *(The) Psychoanalytic Treatment of the Child*. New York: Int. Univ. Press.

———. (1948), *(The) Ego and the Mechanisms of Defense*. London: Hogarth Press.

———. (1958) Adolescence. In: *Psychoanalytic Study of the Child*. New York: Int. Univ. Press. 13: 225-278.

———. (1965), *Normality and Pathology in Childhood*. New York: Int. Univ. Press.

————. (1966), The ideal psychoanalytic institute: a utopia. Paper presented at Chicago Institute for Psychoanalysis, Dec. 21.

Freud, S. (1900), The interpretation of dreams. *Standard Edition of the Complete Psychological Works of . . . ,* 4 and 5. London: Hogarth Press, 1962.

————. (1905), Fragment of an analysis of a case of hysteria. *Standard Edition,* 10: 5-148.

————. (1909), Analysis of a phobia in a five-year-old boy. *Standard Edition,* 10: 5-148.

————. (1911a), Formulations on two principles of mental functioning. *Standard Edition,* 12: 213-226.

————. (1911b), Psychoanalytic notes on an autobiographical account of a case of paranoia. *Standard Edition,* 12: 3-82.

————. (1912), The dynamics of the transference. *Standard Edition,* 12: 97-108.

————. (1913a), On beginning the treatment. *Standard Edition,* 12: 123-124.

————. (1913)b, On psychoanalysis. *Standard Edition,* 12: 207-211.

————. (1914a), On narcissism: an introduction. *Standard Edition,* 14: 73-102.

————. (1914a), Recommendations to physicians practicing psychoanalysis. *Standard Edition,* 12: 111-120.

————. (1914b), Remembering, repeating and working through. *Standard Edition,* 12: 145-156.

————. (1915a), Observations on transference-love. *Standard Edition,* 12: 157-171.

————. (1915b), On the history of an infantile neurosis. *Standard Edition,* 14: 7-123.

————. (1916), Introductory lectures on psychoanalysis (Part III). *Standard Edition,* 16: 243-463.

————. (1921), Group psychology and the analysis of the ego. *Standard Edition,* 18: 69-143.

_____. (1923), The ego and the id. *Standard Edition,* 19: 12-66.

———. (1923), Remarks on the theory and practice of dream interpretation. *Standard Edition,* 19: 12-59.

———. (1925-26), On the question of lay analysis. *Standard Edition,* 20: 179-258.

———. (1926), Inhibitions, symptoms and anxieties. *Standard Edition,* 20: 77-175.

———. (1930), Beyond the pleasure principle. *Standard Edition,* 18: 7-66.

———. (1933), Civilization and its discontents. *Standard Edition,* 21: 64-147.

———. (1933), Metapsychological supplement to the Theory of dreams. In *Collected Papers of S. Freud.* London: Hogarth Press, 1933.

———. (1938), *The Basic Writings of Sigmund Freud.* New York: Random House.

———. (1940), *An Outline of Psychoanalysis.* New York: Norton, 1949.

———. (1954), *The Origins of Psychoanalysis.* Letters to Wilhelm Fliess, Drafts and Notes: New York: Basic Books, 1954.

———. (1965), *General Introduction to Psychoanalysis.* New York: Simon & Schuster.

———. & Breuer, J. (1895), Studies on hysteria. *Standard Edition,* 2: 3-305.

Fromm, E. (1947), *Man for Himself: An Inquiry into the Psychology of Ethics.* New York: Rinehart & Co.

Fromm-Reichman, F. (1952), Some aspects of psychoanalytic psychotherapy with schizophrenics. In: *Psychotherapy with Schizophrenics,* ed. Brody, E. & Redlich, F. New York: Int. Univ. Press.

Gitelson, M. (1952), The emotional position of the analyst in the psychoanalytic situation. *Int. J. Psychoanal,* 33: 1-10.

Glover, E. (1949), *Psychoanalysis* (2nd Ed.) New York: Staples Press.

———. (1955), *The Technique of Psychoanalysis*. London: Bailliere, Tindall & Cox.

———. (1956), *On the Early Development of Mind*. New York: Int. Univ. Press.

Greenson, R. (1958), Variations in psychoanalytic technique. *Int. J. Psychoanal*, 39: 1.

———. (1967), *The Technique and Practice of Psychoanalysis*. New York: Int. Univ. Press.

Grinstein, A. (1974), *On Sigmund Freud's Dreams*. Detroit: Wayne Univ. Press.

Hartmann, H., Lowenstein, R., & Kris, E. (1949), Notes on the theory of aggression. In: *Psychoanal. St. of the Child*, Vol. 4. New York: Int. Univ. Press.

Hendrick, I. (1931), Ego defense and the mechanism of oral rejection in schizophrenics: psychoanalysis of a prepsychotic case. *Int. J. Psychoanal.*, 12: 298-325.

Hill, L. B. (1955), *Psychotherapeutic Intervention in Schizophrenia*. Chicago: Univ. of Chicago Press.

Jones, E. and Trilling, L. (1948), *What Is Psychoanalysis?* Westport, Conn.: Greenwood Press.

Jung, C. (1936), *The Psychology of Dementia Praecox*. New York: Nervous and Mental Disease Pub. Co.

Kernberg, O. (1965), Notes on countertransference. *J. Amer. Psychoanal. Assoc.,* 13: 38-56.

Klein, M. (1952), The origins of transference. *Int. J. Psychoanal.*, 33: 433.

———. (1948), Symposium on child analysis. *Contributions to Psychoanalysis*, 1921-1945. London: Hogarth Press, pp. 152-184.

Kohut, H. (1971), *Analysis of the Self.* New York: Int. Univ. Press.

Lagache, D. (1953), Some aspects of transference. *Int. J. Psychoanal.* 34: 1-10.

LeBoyer, Frederick. (1973), Born happy. New York: *Vogue Magazine*, July.

Little, M. (1958), On delusional transference. *Int. J. Psychoanal.*, 39: 134-138.

————. (1957), The analyst's total response to his patient's needs. *Int. J. Psychoanal.*, 38: 240-254.

Meadow, P. (1974), Research method for investigating the effectiveness of psychoanalytic technique. *Psychoanal. Rev.*, 61(1): 79-94.

————. (1970), The relative effectiveness of two educational techniques used in the extinction of maladaptive responses which block learning. *Dissertation Abstracts Intl.*, 31(2): 1-97.

Meerloo, J. & Coleman Nelson, M. (1951), The transference function. A study of normal and pathological transference. *Psychoanal. Rev.*, 38: 205-221.

Menninger, K. (1945), *The Human Mind.* 3rd ed. New York: Harcourt Brace.

Nagelberg, L. & Spotnitz, H. (1958), Strengthening the ego through the release of frustration-aggression. *Amer. J. Orthophyschiat.*, 28: 794-801.

Nagelberg, L., Spotnitz, H., & Feldman, Y. (1953), The attempt at healthy insulation in the withdrawn child. *Amer. J. Orthopsychiat.*, 23: 238-252.

Nelson, M. Coleman. (1956), Externalization of the toxic introject. *Psychoanal. Rev.*, 43(2): 235-242.

Nunberg, H. (1948), The course of the libidinal conflict in a case of schizophrenia. In: *Practice and Theory of Psychoanalysis.* New York: Nerv. Ment. Dis. Mono., no. 74.

———— & Federn, E., eds. (1962) *Minutes of the Vienna Psychoanalytic*

Society. Vol. 1. New York: Int. Univ. Press, 19th meeting.

Perls, F., Hefferline, R., & Goodman, P. (1951), *Gestalt Therapy.* New York: Julian Press.

Racker, H. (1957), The meaning and uses of countertransference. *Psychoanal. Quart.*, 2: 303-357.

Reich, Annie. (1951), On countertransference. *Int. J. Psychoanal.*, 32: 25-31.

Reich, W. (1949), *Character Analysis* (Trans. P. Wolfe). New York: Orgone Inst. Press.

Reik, T. (1935), *Surprise and the Psychoanalyst: On the Conjecture and Comprehension of Unconscious Processes.* New York: Dutton.

———. (1948), *Listening with the Third Ear.* New York: Farrar Straus.

———. (1949), *From Thirty Years with Freud.* New York: Int. Univ. Press.

———. (1952), *The Secret Self.* New York: Farrar Straus.

Ribble, M. A. (1965), *The Rights of Infants.* New York: Columbia Univ. Press.

Rosen, J. L. (1953), *Direct Analysis.* New York: Grune & Stratton.

———. (1963), *The Concept of Early Maternal Environment in Direct Psychoanalysis.* Doylestown, Pa.: Doylestown Foundation.

Rosenfeld, H. A. (1947), Analysis of a schizophrenic state with depersonalization. *Int. J. Psychoanal.*, 28: 130-139.

———. (1964), On the psychopathology of narcissism. *Int. J. Psychoanal.* 45: 333-347.

Schlesinger, Benno. (1964), *Higher Cerebral Functions and Their Clinical Disorders.* New York: Grune & Stratton.

Searles, H. F. (1965), *Collected Papers on Schizophrenia and Related Subjects.* New York: Int. Univ. Press.

Sechehaye, M. A. (1956), *A New Psychotherapy in Schizophrenia.* New York: Grune & Stratton.

Spitz, R. (1965), *The First Year of Life.* New York: Int. Univ. Press.

Spotnitz, H. (1949), Emotional induction: a consideration of its influence on the process of emotional evolution. Paper presented at the *Am. Psychiat. Assoc.*

———. (1952), A psychoanalytic view of resistance in groups. *Int. J. Grp. Psychoth.*, 2: 3-9.

———. (1955-56), The prophecies of Tiresias. *Psychonal.*, 4(2): 37-43.

———. (1957), The borderline schizophrenic in group psychotherapy. *Int. J. Grp. Psychoth.*, 7: 155-174.

———. (1961a), *The Couch and the Circle: A Story of Group Psychotherapy.* New York: Alfred A. Knopf.

———. (1961b), The narcissistic defense in schizophrenia. *Psychoanal. & Psychoanal. Rev.*, 48: 24-42.

———. (1961c), The third psychiatric revolution. Lecture presented at *Cooper Union Forum*, Oct. 25.

———. (1962), The need for insulation in the schizophrenic personality. *Psychoanal. & Psychoanal. Rev.*, 49(3): 3-25.

———. (1963), The toxoid response. *Psychoanal. Rev.*, 50: 611-624. [c. New York: Stuyvesant Clinic Psychol. Dept. mono. 3: 26-39.]

———. (1965), Symposium on: Resistance of the noncommunicating patient in the group. Unpublished paper presented at *Inst. for the Crippled and Disabled*, Jan.

———. (1967a), The maturational interpretation. In: *Use of Interpretation in Treatment*, ed. E. Hammer. New York: Grune & Stratton, pp. 107-109.

———. (1967b), Techniques for the resolution of the narcissistic defense. In: *Psychoanalytic Techniques*, ed. B. Wolman. New York: Basic Books, pp. 273-289.

———. (1968a), The management and mastery of resistance in group psychotherapy. *J. Grp. Psychoanal.*, 2: 5-22.

———. (1968b), The monopolizer in the group–patient or therapist. Unpublished paper presented at the *Wolverine State Psychotherapy Society*. Detroit, May 8.

————. (1969a), Psychoanalytic therapy of aggression in groups. Unpublished paper presented at *Nassau Neuropsychiatric Society*. Garden City, Apr. 15.

————. (1969b), *Modern Psychoanalysis of the Schizophrenic Patient*. New York: Grune & Stratton.

————. (1969c), Resistance phenomena in group psychotherapy, an overview. In: *Group Therapy Today*. ed., H. M. Ruitenbeck. New York: Atherton Press, pp. 203-221.

————. (1971), Comparison of different types of group psychotherapy. In: *Comprehensive Group Psychotherapy,* eds. H. I. Kaplan & B. J. Sadock. Baltimore: Williams & Wilkins, pp. 72-103.

————. (1971-1975), Training and supervising the modern psychonanalyst. Presented at the *Distinguished Guest Lecturer Series* at Manhattan Center for Advanced Psychoanalytic Studies.

————. (1972), Constructive emotional interchange in adolescence. In: *Progress in Group and Family Therapy*, eds. C. J. Sager & H. S. Kaplan. New York: Brunner/Mazel, pp. 737-746.

———— & Nagelberg, L. (1960), A preanalytic technique for resolving the narcissistic defense. *Psychiatry.*, 23: 193-197.

———— & Feldman, Y. (1956), Ego reinforcement in the schizophrenic child. *Amer. J. Orthopsychiat., 26:* 146-164 146-164.

Stern, Max. (1938), Psychoanalytic investigation of and therapy in the borderline group of neuroses. *Psychoanal. Quart.,* 7: 467-468.

Stone, L. (1954), The widening scope of indications for psychoanalysis. *J. Amer. Psychoanal. Assn.*, 2: 567-594.

Velikovsky, I. (1949), Freud's dreams. *Psychoanal. Rev.*, Winter.

Waelder, R. (1960), *Basic Theory of Psychoanalysis*, New York: Int. Univ. Press.

———. (1925), The psychoses–their mechanisms and accessibility to influence. *Int. J. Psychoanal.*, 6: 259-281.

Weiss, E. (1960), *The Structure and Dynamics of the Human Mind.* New York: Grune & Stratton.

———. (1963-64), Vicissitudes of internalized objects in paranoid schizophrenia and manic depressive states. *Psychoanal. Rev.*, 50: 59-73.

Wilson, C. (1967), *The Outsider.* New York: Dell Books.

Winnicott, D. W. (1958), Hate in the countertransference. In: *Collected Papers.* New York: Basic Books.

———. (1965), *The Maturational Processes and the Facilitating Environment: Studies in the Theory of Emotional Development.* New York: Int. Univ. Press.

Zilboorg, G. (1931), The deeper layers of schizophrenic psychoses. *Amer. J. Psychiat.*, 88: 493-511.

Index

AUTHOR INDEX

SUBJECT INDEX

active technique, (Ferenczi) 147, 148

affect, 59

aggression (aggressive or destructive impulses/wishes), 14, 17, 18, 19, 21, 22, 37, 42, 43, 44, 49, 51, 61, 62, 65, 67, 70, 74, 86, 87, 88, 131, 140, 144, 158, 159, 222

sadism, 21

agoraphobia, 69, 70, 72

alcoholism, 202

analysis, 132, 134, 139, 142, 147

analysand, 127

Anna O. (Bertha Pappenheim), 26, 31, 81, 82

annihilation, 52, 71, 116, 158

anorexia, 62

anxiety, 42, 44, 79

analyst's, 52, 55

appointment time, 150, 172, 180

association (free), 99, 100, 101, 156

See also dreams

aural impressions, 63

Autobiographical Study (An), 18

Beyond the Pleasure Principle, 48

blocks, 13, 17

body language, 78

bottled-up rage, 91, 177, 178

See also aggression

breast, 21, 58, 103, 119, 120, 121, 122, 163, 165, 202

cancer, 123, 133, 208

castration, 118

catatonic, 53, 57, 58

catharsis, 43

cathexis, 22, 58, 62, 74, 158

Civilization and Its Discontents, 38

classical analysis, 28, 62, 90, 156

claustrophobia, 69, 70, 71, 72

cognitive functions, 98

commands (*see* interventions)

communication, 137, 138, 159

inappropriate, 90

compliance, 152

compulsion to repeat (repetition compulsion), 53, 65, 87, 89, 142, 143, 144, 174

confrontation (*see* interpretation, interventions)

contact function, 85, 89, 148, 149, 150, 159, 161, 162, 168, 169, 173, 180, 184, 192, 203, 215

contagion (emotional), 76, 77, 78, 80, 83, 84, 86, 128

See also transmission of feelings

induction, 75

contract (analytic), 150

cooperation (in analysis), 152

couch (use in analysis), 17, 71, 80, 87, 127, 152, 153, 160

countertransference, 29, 68, 80, 81, 82, 86, 123, 163, 164, 174, 213

induced, 83, 89, 133, 188

narcissistic, 75, 193, 214

negative narcissistic, 214

objective, 83, 84, 86, 174

resistance, 93

subjective, 84, 133, 134

cure, 17, 30, 128, 142, 143, 147, 174

See also maturity